Really?

What's Gone Wrong and Why

How Not to Read the Bible

Brian Cockell

Table of Contents

Copyright

Brian Cockell

website at www.thenarrowway.ca
First Printing: November 2021
ISBN 978-1-7771118-4-7

To my wonderful spirit-filled wife, Fonda. The love of my life and partner in Christ. Her passion and commitment to our Lord Jesus Christ and the Holy Scriptures are my inspiration and Joy. May Jesus, our Lord, continue to keep and guide you until we are called, any day now, to the Marriage Supper of the Lamb, to our Savior, to our King!

PREFACE

The year was 2017. I fulfilled the role of Chief Operating Officer, bringing home a mid-6-figure income from one of Canada's largest private companies. Surrounded by corporate corruption, greed, and moral decay daily, I came to realize my life choices were not aligning with my Christian faith and the values and morals I held.

During this period, Fonda (my wife) and I lived on a 100-acre farm. We ran a home-based skincare business, raised goats protected by 8 Maremma sheepdogs, and managed a bee apiary on our property to create goat's milk and beeswax for our products.

Fonda and I both decided enough was enough. We found ourselves firmly rooted in the world. Although we deeply loved the Lord, read the Word, prayed, went to church weekly, preached, and led a weekly bible study in our home, we knew we had to make a change. We believe we are in the season of our Lord's return for his church and that one day soon; we will hear the trumpet call ushering us up to be with our Lord. When we considered the below scripture, we found ourselves looking at each other with concern.

(Matthew 25:21) *"His master replied, 'Well done, good and faithful servant! You have been faithful with a few things; I will put you in charge of many things. Come and share your master's happiness!"*

We asked ourselves, "When we stand before the Lord will we hear the words 'Well done, good and faithful servant'"? Our answer was no!

It was time to make the change we both knew we needed and required. We had to remove both feet from the world and dive headfirst into our faith and dedication to our Lord. Our desire and calling were to serve Jesus and enter into full-time ministry. We did not know what that looked like at the time. However, Fonda and I left our jobs, sold most of our possessions, sold our farm, and moved off-the-grid to an unorganized territory in the deep North of Ontario. Today, 2021, we continue to run our skincare business from the bush, and our eight puppies are now pets rather than working dogs.

You have in your hands the culmination and result of the above changes in our life. This work is my first Christian book and the beginning of my journey to teach and preach God's Word full-time. May you be blessed as you read through this book. May your faith and dedication be strengthened in Jesus Christ.

A servant of Jesus Christ,
Brian Cockell

INTRODUCTION

Why did I write this book? Why should you have any interest in this book?

Is it just me, or is there an unprecedented expeditious meteoric change happening in our world and society beyond measure and speed? As I look around at our world today, something is and has drastically changed and continues to change daily.

As an Evangelical Christian living in the last days, I should not be surprised at witnessing rapid change and degradation in our society, the church, and the world at large. Knowing it is coming is easy to grasp as these events are foretold in scripture. Watching it happen is another story. With this rate of change, even tomorrow is going to look different than today.

On the ecological side of the ledger, the world is experiencing unprecedented earthquakes, floods, droughts, wildfires, natural disasters, pestilence, disease, famine, and the list goes on. We are bystanders to these events without a lot to say in the matter. We are witnessing God's hand at work. Naysayers will point out that we have always had these events with us. They fail to point out the drastic increase in quantity and intensity of each item above.

(A topic I explore in my book "SO SORRY! – You're Not Going to Save it")

The Word of God prescribes these events in the end times and should be no surprise to us today as we witness the fulfilment of God's prophetic Word. These events will continue to increase in quantity and severity as we march toward God's removal of the Restrainer and the Lord's return for his church. Buckle-up, it is going to get bumpy.

On the societal side of the ledger, we find ourselves in the most unprecedented times in humanity's short, chaotic history. The advent of 'Social Justice' is just the tip of the iceberg in a society marching towards and teetering on the brink of collapse. The state of humankind should also not surprise the faithful born-again Christian as we march towards God's ultimate and righteous judgement of the generations and nations.

Democratic governments, if you can call them that anymore, are consolidating power, suppressing free speech, overreaching their electoral and constitutional authority, and expeditiously removing the population's civil and religious rights around the democratic world.

Moral decay, the breakdown of the nuclear family, societal collapse, drug and alcohol dependencies, spiritual disintegration, rampant sexual immorality and hedonism, replacing natural relationships with unnatural ones, gender neutrality or choice, and this list goes on and on now required to be embraced. The repugnancy of what we witness and are expected to adopt, "or else," is an all-out assault on our morality, sensibilities and God. Ultimately the well-being of those who oppose this new world order will be threatened. We already see those who oppose this "New Normal" vilified and labelled the scourge of today's society.

Most distressing is the infiltration of this moral and spiritual decay within the church. False teachers and false prophets are spreading a false gospel, deceiving millions. Congregants passively sit in the pews or watch social media channels, listening to this garbage as sheep being led to the slaughter.

Behaviours not too far in the distant past once considered evil, immoral and unconscionable are today regarded as good, acceptable and the new standard of society. Dissenters, or those who oppose this new normal, are belittled, discouraged, and charged with hate speech. Laws have started to be proposed and implemented to reward evil, lawlessness, and immorality and punish what was once good, pure and just.

I hear you saying, "Brian, that is all well and good, but what does any of that have to do with learning how to interpret, understand, read, memorize my Bible, and apply it to my life?" The answer is everything. We did not wake up today to find ourselves all of a sudden in this new dystopian reality. The change has been gradual and infesting our society for the past number of decades. The causality of this change is directly related to our departure from God and his Word.

The law of "cause and effect" has been our greatest adversary. Well, Satan and his minions are, of course, our greatest adversary. He is the author and instigator of the causes of our downfall. The causes are removing God, his Word, and prayer from our institutions and lives. Allowing false teachers and prophets to infiltrate the church, deceiving many in the Christian community, and departing from sound doctrine to hear whatever itching ears want to hear.

The effects are a broken, immoral society without God, filled with many deceived people claiming Christ, who will not be joining us in heaven. We will explore what this looks like as we move through this book and learn how to correctly interpret and understand the scriptures. We will explore how to apply God's Word to our lives, knowing without a doubt for the genuine believer that salvation is at hand, and we will soon meet our Lord in the air when he calls.

Chapter One
WHO IS THIS GOD?

From where does the concept of God come? How do we know there is a God and he exists? Throughout the ages, the mortal world has had many definitions or feelings of the "One" God, known as monotheism or the "Plurality" of gods, known as polytheism.

Some will tell us that god is a feeling or an emotional state of being. You will hear from others that god is a force within nature. You often hear the term "Mother Nature" thrown around, purported to be the instigating "force" of natural events. Still, others will tell you that God is simply a characterization of good versus evil, morality versus immorality. Atheists, those who outright reject God's existence, will say to you that God is a fairytale and does not exist.

Throughout the ages, god has purportedly existed within, and animated from, inanimate lifeless objects called idols. Others have assigned gods their false deity through and of constellations. Think of the Greek gods. You will find claims of god as animal spirits or earthly objects built upon one another to represent a deity or the sun, moon, earth, water, or sky. The common thread is that these objects become false idles, powerless deities of worship and prayer.

The above two paragraphs are a tiny sampling of misguided beliefs of who and what God is, fabricated throughout the ages. These beliefs taught by those grossly deceived or outright blaspheming heretics lead people to their ultimate doom and eternal separation from the one true God. Correctly interpreting and handling the Word of Truth, the Bible, will quickly show these concepts are not within God's Word, and we should have nothing to do with any of them.

Our first introduction to the one true God, reciting the beginning of our story almost 6000 years ago, predates all of the above false concepts. We are introduced to the monotheistic true God for the first time in the first scroll of five scrolls known in the Hebrew language as the Tora or in the Greek language the Pentateuch. Today, these five scrolls are also known as the Five Books of Moses. We know them best as the first five books of the Bible. The book of Genesis is the first of these five books. The literal meaning of Genesis is "In the beginning."

We find our first introduction to God in the very first sentence of the very first book of the Bible.

(Genesis 1:1)
In the beginning God created the heavens and the earth.
(NKJV)

This very first verse of the book of Genesis places God in existence before creating the heavens and the earth. He was pre-existent before this event of creation. The beginning represents the earth's and the universe's historical origin and creation and all that resides within it—the beginning of the heavens and the earth created by our Eternal God.

This beginning in the first chapter of Genesis then gives an account of the first six days of creation, including the origin of all life and the creation of man. When God was finished His work of creation at the end of the sixth day, He declared before His rest on the seventh day:

(Genesis 1:31)
"And God saw everything that he had made, and behold, it was very good. And there was evening and there was morning, the sixth day." (ESV)

These papyrus scrolls, generally accepted as being written or dictated by Moses between 1450-1410 B.C., were our first "written" introduction to God. Our chapter title begs the question, "Who is this God?" Rather than seek our answer from the musings of fallible men or women, we can better find our answer in the infallible, inspired Word of God we call the Bible. God unequivocally tells us directly who he is and what our position is under his authority. Let's take a look at who God declares himself to be through the lens of scripture.

God is first Triune. There is one God in three personages, God the Father, God the Son and God the Holy Spirit. We call this union the Godhood or the Holy Trinity. Tri means three, and unity means one in a union, Trinity. You will not find the word trinity in the Bible. However, you will find over 30 verses where all three members of the Godhood are mentioned in unison. There are hundreds upon hundreds of passages that support all three personages of God throughout the scriptures. As an example:

(Matthew 28:19)
"Therefore go and make disciples of all nations, baptizing them in the name of the Father and of the Son and of the Holy Spirit…."

(John 15:23)

"But when the Helper comes [The Holy Spirit], whom I will send to you from the Father, the Spirit of truth, who proceeds from the Father [God], he will bear witness about me [Jesus]...." (AMP)

The Godhood is not three Gods coexisting but rather one God in three personages. The Trinity is one of the most misunderstood theologies within the Word of God and one of the hardest to grasp. One way to help you understand it is to consider an analogy.

One analogy would be to consider water. Water comes in three forms, a liquid, a gas, and a solid or liquid, steam, and ice. Each one is distinct from the other, but all three continue to be 100% water. It is essential to understand the Trinity or Godhood to examine how God describes himself throughout the scriptures.

It is beyond the scope of this book to write a complete apologetic on the Godhood. You can find many excellent books dedicated to teaching on the Trinity written by theologically sound authors, and don't forget the Bible itself.

Let's look at some of the names taken or proclaimed for each member of the Trinity. Knowing what some of the names are will help us see the oneness of God in His three personages.

The Names of God

There are over 100 names for God in the Bible, either ascribed by Him or attributed to Him. Here are some of the names God has given himself. He instructs the Israelites to refer to him by these names and, by extension, everyone else for now and forever.

(Exodus 3:13-15)
"Then Moses said to God, "Behold, when I come to the Israelites and say to them, 'The God of your fathers (ancestors) has sent me to you,' and they say to me, 'What is His name?' What shall I say to them?" God said to Moses, "I AM WHO I AM"; and He said, "You shall say this to the Israelites, 'I AM has sent me to you.'" Then God also said to Moses, "This is what you shall say to the Israelites, 'The LORD, the God of your fathers, the God of Abraham, the God of Isaac, and the God of Jacob (Israel), has sent me to you.' This is My Name forever, and this is My memorial [name] to all generations." (AMP)

The English "I AM" is translated from YHWH. These four characters have no known pronunciation in modern times and are too reverent to be uttered or spoken by Jewish tradition. From YHWH, we get one of God's best-known and revered names of Yahweh. The name we use today in English, "The Lord," or "God," is the translation from the Hebrew name Adonai.

The Names of Jesus
(Luke 1:30-31)
"The angel said to her, "Do not be afraid, Mary, for you have found favor with God. Listen carefully: you will conceive in your womb and give birth to a son, and you shall name Him Jesus."

(Luke 2:21)
"At the end of eight days, when He was to be circumcised, He was named Jesus, the name given [to Him] by the angel [Gabriel] before He was conceived in the womb." (AMP)

In the sixth month of Mary's pregnancy, God sent the angel Gabriel to Mary and Joseph before the birth of Jesus to declare God himself has assigned a name to Jesus. Jesus is translated from the Hebrew name Yeshua. The name Yeshua means salvation.

As per Cruden's Concordance published in 1737, there are 198 names for Jesus throughout scripture within the combined Old and New Testaments.

Names help describe the attributes and characteristics of God. Each name fits wonderfully into the tenants and truths of scripture as we unfold the story of God and His creation. Here are a couple more examples to help understand how his titles fit into the roles He has assigned to himself. This first example from the Prophet Isaiah ascribes four names to Jesus in one verse.

(Isaiah 9:6)
"For to us a Child shall be born, to us a Son shall be given; And the government shall be upon His shoulder, And His name shall be called Wonderful Counselor, Mighty God, Everlasting Father, Prince of Peace." (AMP)

(Matthew 1:23)
"Behold, the virgin shall conceive and bear a son, and they shall call his name Immanuel (which means, God with us)." (ESV)

The Names of The Holy Spirit

Thirty-two names are attributed to the Holy Spirit, the third member of the Trinity. Like God the Father and Jesus Christ the Son, The Holy Spirit's names are linked to his aspect, characteristics, and ministry to the world. He is generally referred to as "The Spirit," The "Holy Spirit," the "Spirit of God," the "Eternal Spirit," and many more.

Ok, that was a very abridged look at the Triune God and how He is named in the scriptures. Let's continue with our look at what God has to say about himself from His own words to help answer our question, "Who is This God?" our chapter title asks.

Almighty, All-Powerful, All-Knowing

(Revelation 1:8)
"I am the Alpha and the Omega [the Beginning and the End]," says the Lord God, "Who is [existing forever] and Who was [continually existing in the past] and Who is to come, the Almighty [the Omnipotent, the Ruler of all]." (AMP)

(Genesis 17:1)
"When Abram was ninety-nine years old, the Lord appeared to him and said, "I am God Almighty; Walk [habitually] before Me [with integrity, knowing that you are always in My presence], and be blameless and complete [in obedience to Me]." (AMP)

(Hebrews 1:3)
The Son is the radiance and only expression of the glory of [our awesome] God [reflecting God's Shekinah glory, the Light-being, the brilliant light of the Divine], and the exact representation and perfect imprint of His [Father's] essence, and upholding and maintaining and propelling all things [the entire

physical and spiritual universe] by His powerful Word [carrying the universe along to its predetermined goal]. When He [Himself and no other] had [by offering Himself on the cross as a sacrifice for sin] accomplished purification from sins and established our freedom from guilt, He sat down [revealing His completed work] at the right hand of the Majesty on high [revealing His Divine authority], (AMP)

(Revelation 1:18)
and the Ever-living One [living in and beyond all time and space]. I died, but see, I am alive forevermore, and I have the keys of [absolute control and victory over] death and of Hades (the realm of the dead). (AMP)

(Colossians 1:17)
"And He Himself existed and is before all things, and in Him all things hold together. [His is the controlling, cohesive force of the universe.]" (AMP)

God describes himself as the Alpha and the Omega, the first and last letters in the Greek alphabet, the beginning and the end. He always was, He is, and He always will be. "The Almighty" denotes God as Omnipotent, meaning an all-powerful supreme being. "The Almighty" also signifies omniscience, meaning all-knowing. There never was, or there never will be another being as the Almighty.

The entire physical world, universe and all that is in it, including you and me, is held together and continues to function by the power of God and his Word. What a magnificent picture and comfort it is to know our Creator cares for each of us daily. He cares so much that he sacrificed his own Son to pay the price for our purification and forgiveness of the sin we all carry due to our fallen state that is prodded on by the great deceiver Satan. The big question is, do you accept that sacrifice by confessing Jesus as Lord and Savior? (More on this in subsequent chapters)

God exists outside of time and space as we know it. He is omnipresent, meaning His presence is everywhere and always has been. He has power and control over life and death and holds complete overall divine authority over the physical and spiritual realms.

(1 Peter 1:15)
"But like the Holy One who called you, be holy yourselves in all your conduct [be set apart from the world by your godly character and moral courage];" (AMP)

God, In addition to all of the above, is Holy. He is righteous, full of goodness and mercy, and requires our complete devotion and exaltation. By extension,

God instructs us to walk blameless and holy before Him, exhibiting godly character in the world but not of the world. We are required to live our lives in a godly manner pleasing to Him and an example to others.

That, again, is a relatively quick look at some of the character and attributes of God. We could spend an entire series of books exploring who God is; however, I want to move rather quickly into the substance and purpose of this book, but I think that helps us to answer our chapter title's question, 'Who is this God?"

God is the mighty Creator and sustainer of the heavens and the earth and everything in them by his Word. He is loving, all-powerful, all-knowing, ever-present, righteous, sovereign, Holy, merciful, faithful and just. God is the King of Kings and Lord of Lords, and everything and everyone is subject to and under God's authority whether they like it or not.

That is a mouthful. How do we really know all this to be true? There are, at a minimum, three answers to this question. Let's take a look at them one by one.

(Romans 2:15)
"who show the work of the law written in their hearts, their conscience also bearing witness, and between themselves their thoughts accusing or else excusing them."

Firstly, in Romans 2:11-15, Paul, the author of this book, deals with the Jewish Law and how it does or does not affect Jews and gentiles (Non-Jewish People). The premise is, God has created us in his image. Because of this, God's Laws are written within our hearts, as he says they are, whether we like it or not. We all have the innate knowledge of good and evil imprinted within us. By extension, we have the knowledge of our Creator within us. Some accept his presence. Some do not. Because someone rejects this truth, it does not mean it is not there, and there is no God.

As a result of our innate knowledge of God, when we step outside the bounds and providence that God has placed us under, we are morally and consciously accused of our wrongdoing, whether we are believers or not. The difference between believers and non-believers is that the believer knows that we have broken God's Law when we sin by conviction from the Holy Spirit and the Law written within us. We then repent and seek God's forgiveness for this sin; he forgives us our trespasses.

The unbeliever wages an eternal battle attempting to excuse and deny the truth of God's existence and his Laws written within them. The unbeliever denies their failing under God's law, and when they sin, they suppress the conviction of the Holy Spirit.

The simple fact is we know God exists by our internal convictions, knowledge of good and evil and the prompting of our spirit when we step outside of God's natural Law. The believer accepts this fact. The unbeliever wages war against themselves, doing the best they can to deny the inevitable truth of God. See also (Romans 1:32)

(Psalm 19:1-4)
The heavens declare the glory of God;
*   the skies proclaim the work of his hands.*

(Romans 1:20)
Since the creation of the world, God's invisible qualities—his eternal power and divine nature—have been clearly seen, being understood from what has been made, so that people are without excuse.

Secondly, the entirety of God's creation speaks to His glory, eternal power, divine nature and loudly proclaims the works of his hands. You don't need to go much further than simply looking up. God's created splendor leaves you standing in awe. No, there was no big bang. There was no evolutionary process that spawned the universe. The universe and all that is in it is God's creation, His handy work as he claims.

If God's creation of the heavens and the earth is not enough to get you excited about the Creator and His creation, take a look at yourself. Evolution is not the answer. There are more holes in the evolutionary theories than in swiss cheese. If reptiles evolved from fish, why are there still fish? If man evolved from apes, why are there still apes running around? Where are all the transitional species or the skeletons of such? You don't see them because they don't exist. I could write volumes on the failed theory of evolution, but we will stop there.

The chance of all the species evolving separate and distinct, male and female, is 1 in infinity or, better yet, mathematically impossible. We are a created being. The only decision left is who created you and all the living things of the earth. The only answer is the God of the Bible. He created mankind from the dust of the earth just as he said he did and left no excuse for any other explanation. You don't have to look any further than the created wonder you are.

(Hebrews 4:12)
For the Word of God is living and active, sharper than any two-edged sword, piercing to the division of soul and of spirit, of joints and of marrow, and discerning the thoughts and intentions of the heart. (ESV)

(2 Timothy 3:16-17)
All Scripture is breathed out by God and profitable for teaching, for reproof, for correction, and for training in righteousness, that the man of God may be complete, equipped for every good work. (ESV)

The third way God reveals himself to us is through His written Word the Bible. God describes His Word as God-breathed, living and active, meaning it comes directly from God through God-inspired men and is something to be interacted with. The Word does not expire or go out of date. It is the same today as it was yesterday and will remain so tomorrow. The Word dives deep within us when we study and meditate on it, giving us comfort in our victories and correction in our failures.

These are the three main areas we learn of God and his existence. Being His created, His creation, and His Word. If you are following a different god, you have been deceived. If you have knowledge of the one true God but have been led astray by false teachers and heretics, it is time to know the one true God and what expectations he has of us. The clock is ticking. Christ will be returning for his true church very soon. Will you be joining us?

Following false teachers, attending church once in a while, Not fellowshipping with those who are genuinely saved, not spending time in prayer, not reading the Word, mishandling the Word, being caught up in and loving the world, walking in perpetual unconfessed and unrepented sin, the list goes on. These are just some of the signs of trouble and should give you pause if you fall into any of the above categories.

Does anyone in the above category have true salvation? Once saved, always saved, you can not lose your salvation as we will cover. The bigger question and concern is, are those in the categories above genuinely saved in the first place or have they been deceived? Are they just posers fooling themselves and everyone around them?

In the introduction, we took a quick look at the ongoing worsening, sad state of affairs the world finds itself in today. One of the most significant casualties has been the state of the church and its departure from scriptural truth and teaching. How has this happened?

This is what I aim to answer in the following chapters through Biblical analysis. What has happened to the church? What do we do to fix it, or is there even a fix? How does one know they are genuinely saved, and if not, what steps need to be taken to assure the true salvation we seek, knowing without a doubt that we will hear the Lord's call when it comes? Let's dig in and get to the bottom of these answers.

Chapter Two
WHAT IS THE BIBLE?

What is the Bible? No, really, what is the Bible? Besides being the infallible, inspired Word of God as seen in 2 Timothy 3:16-17 above and many other areas of scripture, what is it? I can start by telling you what it is not. It is not a book where you memorize a couple of the popular phrases to throw around to impress your friends to sound "Christiany." It is also not a book to be carried to church each Sunday to impress whoever you think you impress with clear evidence that it is rarely opened. It is not a book to collect dust on your coffee table to convince your visiting friends how spiritual you are.

Ok, great, that hurt. Yes, if you fall into the categories above, it probably did but stay with me. Tomorrow you can fix the errors of today. The only thing on the line here is your eternal salvation or, adversely, your eternal separation from God in Hell, where there will be weeping and gnashing of teeth.

A recent and ongoing annual study by Statista on Bible readership is staggering. This study shows that only 11% of people in 2021 read their Bible each day in the U.S. A whopping 29% of people never read it, and 10% read it less than once per year. Everyone else falls somewhere in between, with the majority of people reading the Bible less than once per month. The Pew Research survey in 2020 shows 65% of people in the U.S. identify themselves as Christians. This number is down from 85% in 1990. Of 65 people out of 100 claiming to be Christian, only 11 read and study the Bible daily. That is a travesty.

The Bible is a collection of 66 books. There are 39 books in the old testament and 27 books in the new testament. The books of the Bible were written on three continents, Asia (modern-day Israel), Egypt (Africa), and cities in Europe. Around 40 different authors wrote the Bible in three different languages, Hebrew, Greek, and Aramaic. The Bible was written over a period of about 1500 to 2000 years. These are some of the facts that make the Bible absolutely unique to any other book ever written.

What makes the Bible so unique and utterly amazing is the complexity and unique challenges of the above. The books of the Bible were written by Kings, prophets, fishermen, scholars, statesmen, shepherds, peasants, and many more. There are no contradictions whatsoever, and the narratives are unified, consistent and without error through all 66 books. Only Divine, supernatural inspiration could have pulled off such a feat. There is no other explanation. Those who will tell you differently are mistaken, misinterpret, or do not understand how to interpret God's Word in context. Throughout this book, we will learn how to correctly handle the Word of Truth and apply it to our daily lives.

The Bible is the oldest book in the history of man. Now, you might say wait a minute, Brian, there is clear evidence and historical records that The Epic of Gilgamesh and others like Homer's Iliad are older than the Bible. This belief is a misnomer. What constitutes a book? Writing systems began to be developed in Mesopotamia way back in 2600 BCE. These early systems began development on stone tablets and then advanced to clay tablets, animal skins, papyrus and copper scrolls.

The challenge with these "First" books is that they were all recorded from the time of writing moving forward. The exception is the Bible. Through divine revelation and the passing down of oral tradition, the Word of God began to be recorded from day one of creation, making it the oldest book ever recorded through the ages.

Between 1450 and 1455 A.D., Johannes Gutenberg invented the first moving type mass printing system. One of the first books the Gutenberg press printed is known today as the Gutenberg Bible. The Guinness Book of World Records records this Bible as the oldest known mass-printed book in existence.

Many ask, how do we know the Bible was passed down and recorded correctly without error? The primary way we know is because God tells us it is. One example we find in Psalm 12.

(Psalm 12:6-7)
"The words of the Lord are pure words,
Like silver tried in a furnace of earth,
Purified seven times.
You shall keep them, O Lord,
You shall preserve them from this generation forever." (NKJV)

Although we need to look no further than the truth of the Word of God, we do know around 381 A.D., the First Council of Constantinople decided what books would be included in the Bible. The work of the Constantinople Council concluded about 50 years of study and debate, including events like the Council of Nicea in 325 A.D. We know St. Jerome, around

400 A.D., assembled all 66 books of the Bible into the 66 books we have today.

Here are some examples of the criteria used to qualify or disqualify a book from appearing in the final selection. Were there discrepancies with other texts, were the books written firsthand or with firsthand knowledge, were the books written within the first century and a half in the case of the New Testament and so on.

Some groups have added 14 books to the original 66. Debate continues whether these 14 books, depending on how they are divided, known as the Apocrypha, should be canonized. Canonized means accepted as authoritative scripture. The original 14 books of the Apocrypha were placed in the middle of the Catholic Bible between the Old and New Testaments. You can still find 7 of them in the Catholic Bible today for 73 books in total.

One incredible testimony to the accuracy of the scriptures happened in 1947 when a couple of Bedouin teenagers happened across a cave on the N.W. shore of the Dead Sea near Khirbet Qumran. In this cave, and a number more caves subsequently found, the Dead Sea Scrolls were unearthed. These scrolls are significant because they are in the range of 1000 years older than the scrolls used by the Constantinople Council of 381 A.D. There were fragments of thirty-eight Old Testament Books and a complete copy of the Isaiah Scroll. All of the scrolls and fragments confirmed the accuracy of the texts from the councils.

In addition to the above, the Bible is the most incredible love story ever told. The love of the Creator for his creation, you and me. A love so deep he sent his only begotten Son to die on the cross to pay the penalty for our sins and prepare a road for our eternal salvation for those that accept and believe in Him. One of the best-known passages of scripture attests to this truth. John 3:16.

(John 3:16)
"For God so loved the world that He gave His only begotten Son, that whoever believes in Him should not perish but have everlasting life." (NKJV)

The Bible is also many other things. The Bible is a book of sacrifice, self-help, saving grace, salvation, sanctification, justification, revelation, history, architecture, mystery, ancestry and genealogy, science and math, a travel journal and much more. It is the best-selling book of all time and the most incredible life-changing book you will ever read.

Some Bible fun facts. There are over 100 million Bibles sold each year, and the Bible has been translated into almost 700 languages. It is estimated by the Bible Society that since 1812 there have been more than 5 billion copies of the Bible printed. The authorized King James Version of the Bible consists of 1189 chapters containing 31,102 verses, 783,137 words and 3,116,480 letter characters. That is a lot of characters. There are over 6500 commands, between 6000 and 8000 prophesies, depending on how you count them taking into account duplicates or confirmations. There are over 1200 promises in the Bible. The shortest verse in the Bible is only two words. John 11:35 "Jesus wept." The oldest living character in the Bible is Noah's grandfather Methusela. He lived to be 969 years old before the flood. The Bible is a fascinating, exciting book full of mysteries and truths to be unravelled.

The Bible is God's owner's manual, a blueprint or a recipe for your life, an instruction book on Holy living pleasing to God. It is the only set of instructions you will ever need. What is a blueprint? A blueprint is a set of written instructions on how to accomplish a task.

You would never find a construction crew building a building without meticulously following the blueprint for its construction. Why do we find the majority of those claiming Christ ignoring the Word of God? Departing from God's word makes no sense to me and starts to help explain how we have ended up in the position this degrading, immoral society finds itself.

In 1 Corinthians 12:12-27, Jesus uses the analogy of the body to describe the church. This analogy is a little longer passage but a fundamental analogy when looking at and seeking to understand God's Word.

(1 Corinthians 12:12-27)
Just as a body, though one, has many parts, but all its many parts form one body, so it is with Christ. For we were all baptized by one Spirit so as to form one body—whether Jews or Gentiles, slave or free—and we were all given the one Spirit to drink. Even so the body is not made up of one part but of many.

Now if the foot should say, "Because I am not a hand, I do not belong to the body," it would not for that reason stop being part of the body. And if the ear should say, "Because I am not an eye, I do not belong to the body," it would not for that reason stop being part of the body. If the whole body were an eye, where would the sense of hearing be? If the whole body were an ear, where would the sense of smell be? But in fact God has placed the parts in the body, every one of them, just as he wanted them to be. If they were all one part, where would the body be? As it is, there are many parts, but one body.

The eye cannot say to the hand, "I don't need you!" And the head cannot say to the feet, "I don't need you!" On the contrary, those parts of the body that seem to be weaker are indispensable, and the parts that we think are less honorable we treat with special honor. And the parts that are unpresentable are treated with special modesty, while our presentable parts need no special treatment. But God has put the body together, giving greater honor to the parts that lacked it, so that there should be no division in the body, but that its parts should have equal concern for each other. If one part suffers, every part suffers with it; if one part is honored, every part rejoices with it. Now you are the body of Christ, and each one of you is a part of it.

God uses this analogy to compare the working of the body to the working of the church. Each member of the body is not very useful without all the other members. Each member of the church, each with their own gifts, completes the church to function as designed. A body or a church is only complete and functioning correctly with all its parts intact and filling the role assigned to each body member.

Using the above analogy applied to God's Word is one of the best ways to describe the working of scripture together as a whole. The body has many working parts; all brought together into a whole to function as designed. The 66 books of scripture are all brought together to work and function as a whole. Together, these books function as intended to tell the Bible's story. The story of what was, what is, what will be, and how we fit into the narrative. The work and declarations of the Old Testament Prophets would mean very little without seeing, as time marched on, the fulfillment of those prophecies in subsequent books as an example.

The word of God is not a collection of mutually distinct passages haphazardly stitched together into paragraphs and books. God was not looking to fill white space to bolster his word count. God has placed, just as with the body, every word, sentence, paragraph and book exactly where it belongs and where he wanted it. Each book, taken on its own, only tells a small piece of a complete narrative. Single Bible passages or sentences taken on their own, out of context, can be twisted into an incorrect interpretation of the text. We see the importance of taking the entirety of the scriptures in Matthew 4:4 as one example. Another excellent example of many is the verse we also quoted earlier from 2 Timothy 3:16-17.

(Matthew 4:4)
"Jesus answered, "It is written: 'Man shall not live on bread alone, but on every word that comes from the mouth of God."

(2 Timothy 3:16-17)
"All Scripture is God-breathed and is useful for teaching, rebuking, correcting and training in righteousness, so that the servant of God may be thoroughly equipped for every good work."

The terms in these verses, "but on every word that comes from the mouth of God" and" All Scripture is God-breathed" gives a clear indication of what we are talking about. The Bible is one complete work and needs to be taken as a whole, not in bits and pieces. The complete narrative of the scripture, what was, what is, and what is to come can only be extracted through the study of the entire work of God's Word.

What God has for you to unravel from the mystery of his Word can only be accomplished through reading and studying all 66 books as a whole taken together in context. These books fit together like a glove revealing the complete narrative of God's plan woven through his complete word for the entirety of his creation, including you and me. Are you spending quality time each day studying the blueprint for your life, God's Word, that He has given you for your life instructions and Holy living? If you are falling short, I suggest today should be the day to rededicate some time each day to the life-saving grace of the Word.

When I talk to people about God's Word, I often hear comments like, "It is too complicated," or "I don't understand it," or "What that guy was preaching makes no sense to me." Or "How am I ever able to know how to interpret that imagery?" These comments are some of the biggest inhibitors keeping people from living in and absorbing the Word of God.

Another common complaint I hear is, "I've been a Christian for ten years now, and all I hear from the pulpit every week is the basic salvation message. Where is the meat of the Gospel, the deep teaching?" Most of the failure comes from two sources. Inadequate and unprepared Bible teachers and some pastors of the day preaching a false Gospel, giving false hope, running around deceiving people.

How do we actually interpret and learn what the Bible has for us? This question is the million-dollar question and the stumbling block for most. When I used to operate in senior executive roles in my prior industry, I would attend morning safety meetings. I used to work in the garbage and recycling industry running north of 2000 garbage and recycling trucks a day. I would become very frustrated right out of the gate at almost every one of these meetings. The morning managers would be instructing the driving teams to get out there and be safe today. They would tell them not to hit anything then send them on their way. Are you kidding me? That is not how you run a safety meeting. What kind of instruction is that? These words are statements with no direction or instruction attached to them.

You run a safety meeting by giving clear training and instruction on the expectation and how to achieve it. "Ok, ladies and gentlemen. The expectation is that you will head out there today and be safe. It is a condition of your employment. You will not injure yourself or others, and you will return your truck at the end of the day without having an incident or accident.

You are required to use your personal protective equipment at all times. Please inspect your equipment for any damage before departing. If any items are damaged, have them replaced by your manager. Complete your circle check, and make sure to check your tire pressure before you get into your truck.

When getting in and out of your truck, you are to use three points of contact. Hand hand foot or foot foot hand. When lifting, bend at the knees and not your back. Inspect all bags for sharps before picking up a bag. Test the weight of the bag before attempting to lift it.

When in your truck, drive the speed limit, keep your eyes moving left center right every 5 seconds, scanning for objects and other vehicles. Check your mirrors every 8 seconds. Leave yourself an out by creating a space cushion around your vehicle and other drivers. Hover your brake when approaching stale yellow lights in preparation to stop if the light does change. Do not stop over the crest of a hill where other drivers can't see you. Keep your cellphone in your pocket unless you are parked in a safe spot with the keys out of the ignition. Now get out there and follow these safety instructions. Failure to do so can cost you or someone else their life. Have a good day, and be safe out there.

That is how you teach and instruct a driving crew to operate safely throughout the day. We have the exact same failures in the church in two areas. Most Pastors and teachers drone off scripture to you without interpretation or proper instruction. Most messages are so shallow, with no meat or deep teaching, you might as well have stayed home and read the Bible yourself. Sure, we are instructed to gather together in fellowship, and it is a strong instruction from scripture. I am not suggesting you should not go to church, but rather, you should be in a Spirit-filled church preaching and adequately teaching the entire Bible.

Does what you experience at church on Sunday morning resemble anything like the scriptural model of fellowship? I am guessing, in not all, but in most circumstances, it does not. We shuffle in, shake a couple of hands, trudge through a couple of songs, listen to an uninspired milk message, a message with little substance, then shuffle out when done and call it a day until next week. If there is no spiritual life within your church, it might be time to seek out a spirit-filled church teaching and preaching God's Word with conviction and truth.

The second and even more distressing turn of events is the false teachers teaching a false gospel leading you like sheep to the slaughter. You would be better off going to a quilting class Sunday morning than listening to another second of the garbage being spewed from the pulpits of this group. The only tool you have to discern against false teaching is a personal and intimate knowledge of the scriptures.

In the next chapter, we will take a slight detour to help us establish a starting point of Biblical interpretation and understanding. Then, in the subsequent chapter, we will tackle reading, learning, and interpreting your Bible correctly. I will teach you how to handle the Word of truth with clear, precise instructions.

From there, we will then learn how to discern against and protect ourselves from false teachers, preachers, Prophets, and outright heretics as described on multiple accounts in the Bible. Those evil-doers are leading people to eternal damnation and separation From God. We will end with the how to's and the importance of memorizing the Word.

Chapter Three
DETOUR

The interpretation and understanding of the scriptures look very different through the lens of a believer versus a non-believer or heretic. We will take a slight detour to help build the case of understanding and interpretation.

When I was a young man, I was a devout atheist and evolutionist in my late teens and early twenties. I had no interest in God or belief in God. I was very antagonistic towards anybody espousing such views. I spent my days heckling, mocking, bullying, and maligning anyone and everyone who ever approached me on the subject of God to the point of belligerence.

To my mind, these Christians were weak-willed people looking for a crutch to hold on to while trying to navigate their mundane lives with their petty problems. When I look at that statement, I have difficulty reconciling it with who I am today. If you had taken a vote back then of the most unlikely person ever to become a Christian, my name would have been at the top of the list. Fortunately for me, God works in loving, mysterious ways and has the patience to deal in grace and patience with someone like I was.

When I was 18, I played Junior A hockey and owned a large plastics business. I drove a fancy sports car with one of the first mobile phones in it the size of a cement block and walked around like the king of the mountain. My personal motto was, I will do what I want when I want, and nobody will stand in my way. If you were going to arm wrestle me, you would have to break my arm before I let you beat me. The word "humility" was not in my vocabulary. It soon became apparent that God had a couple of different ideas for my life than I had.

What I soon learned was, you make a plan for yourself, life makes a plan for you, and then God throws both those plans out the window in favor of His plan. At this point in my life, I was diagnosed with a debilitating disease known as ankylosing spondylitis that had or has no cure. Back then, not a lot was known about this disease. I was told I would be in a wheelchair by the time I was 30 and blind by the time I was 40.

I quickly ended up walking with the help of a cane and would often get stuck in bed for sometimes days at a time. How the mighty fall. I had also met a girl. It turned out her parents were a couple of those Christians. On no! The first time she took me home to meet them, they asked if I was saved. I told them sure; I have a good chunk of money in the bank, and after a gentle correction, things went downhill fast. I was told because I was not saved, I could not date their daughter. Their definition of saved was accepting Jesus as my saviour. Well, that wasn't going to happen.

After some negotiation, we agreed that I would take their Bible, disprove it all, and then take their daughter and be gone. They agreed, game-on. I got myself a Bible and began the task of proving it all wrong. Like any good atheist, not knowing how to read the scriptures, I started at the beginning like any other book. It meant nothing to me. It was full of mumbo jumbo, imagery, symbolism, rules, laws, parables, this thing called salvation and grace, and I won't even get started on revelation. However, what was interesting to me was although I was not on a mission to prove it right, I was unable to prove it wrong. I consider myself a little bit of a scientist and a researcher, so I started to dig a little deeper.

I tested Historical statements and locations against history. Darn, nothing out of place there. I looked at prophecies in regards to Kingdoms, events, timelines, locations and people. Darn again, they all checked out, and a whole bunch of these prophecies happened just as foretold; go figure. I followed the Nation of Isreal's plight through to its rebirth in 1948. Are you kidding me? That rebirth is impossible; nothing in history has ever happened like that, and to think it was foretold way back when. I tested the claims of creation to what I knew of evolution. Oh, oh, that creation story poked several holes in my evolutionary belief. Darn again. I followed the story of Jesus through to his death on the cross and resurrection. According to historical records, it appeared that this guy really existed, and these events happened just as these prophet guys said they would. The Bible did not yet make any sense to me, but the pieces I was pulling out to look at, the individual snippets, were all aligning or happening as the Bible indicated.

Ok, this was not going well. I figured I better immerse myself a little deeper into my quest. I started to go to church. Maybe I could catch them in their lies and be done with this. Nope, all they talked about was the stuff I was already reading and what some of it meant, and they kept giving this altar call thing. I was like, not on your life. Little did I yet understand it was literally my life at stake. My heart was still hard, and the pride of who I thought I was kept me resisting the truth, but I was beginning to lose the battle. Now, what do I do? I had the answer! If I can't beat them through disproof, I will take on this God one-on-one and put him through some tests. Take some of that; how smart I am!

Alright, how am I going to test this God? Perfect, what better test than have Him jump through a couple of hoops for me. Being a smoker at the time, I knew the ideal way to test Him. "Ok, God, if you are there, I have a little test for you to prove it. I will set my cigarette pack up on its end on top of my dresser when I go to bed. Here is an easy task for you. Simply knock it over when I am sleeping, and I will believe you exist. I am sure since you claim you made the universe and all that, you can probably handle this little test." Night one, nothing. Night two, nothing. A week later, nothing. Bah! Well, that backfired because I soon clued in that although I did not get the proof I needed, I also made no headway in disproving His existence either, back to the drawing board. I must have missed the scripture from Luke 4. Oops.

At this point, I was out of answers. I continued reading and studying and going to church. Slowly God began to soften my heart. Eventually, I was sitting in my office one Sunday morning reading the Bible. My foreman came in and asked me what I was reading. I told him the Bible, and he asked if I was religious. My answer was I would be as soon as you leave. He scratched his head and left. I accepted Jesus into my heart, went out to see my foreman, confessed Jesus publicly with my mouth, and became saved that Sunday morning. I immediately threw my cane down, went outside and ran. I ran for 2 hours and never looked back. I am not claiming that I was healed. I am stating that I have not needed to walk with a cane from that day, and the ankylosing spondylitis stopped progressing. I continue with the thorn of back and hip pain and know without a doubt; God has left me with this reminder to walk in humility before him. When I don't, a new jolt of chronic pain quickly puts me back in line.

Why did I tell this story? How does it fit into understanding and interpreting the Bible? It has everything to do with it. Once I confessed Christ as saviour, the study and meditation I had been doing all of a sudden began to fit together like a jigsaw puzzle. What was unknown became known. All the individual pieces of the Word started to come together before my eyes in a breathtaking fashion. It was wonderful. The story's first moral is that you don't tell God to show you, and then you will believe. The correct answer is first to believe in faith, and then God will show you. He has been showing me ever since every day.

The second moral of the above story is the scriptures make it abundantly clear that the unbeliever cannot make heads or tails of the Word of God. To the unbeliever, it is, as I stated above, mumbo jumbo. The unbeliever sees the Word of God as folly. Sure, you might glean some intellectual information from the Word and understand some of the historical contexts. Yes, you might gain head-knowledge of people, places and events. However, you will never experience a spiritual awakening and understand the deeper truths of scripture until you are a believer. How do I know this? Two ways, my own experience, but more importantly, that is what the Bible tells us. Here are just three examples of what the scriptures say about unbelievers' hardened hearts and ignorance.

(Ephesians 4:18)
"They are darkened in their understanding, alienated from the life of God because of the ignorance that is in them, due to their hardness of heart." (ESV)

(2 Corinthians 4:4)
"In their case the god of this world has blinded the minds of the unbelievers, to keep them from seeing the light of the gospel of the glory of Christ, who is the image of God." (ESV)

(1 Corinthians 2:14)
"But the natural [unbelieving] man does not accept the things [the teachings and revelations] of the Spirit of God, for they are foolishness [absurd and illogical] to him; and he is incapable of understanding them, because they are spiritually discerned and appreciated, [and he is unqualified to judge spiritual matters]." (AMP)

The term "hardness of heart" directly references those who do not believe in God and his Word. Those with hardened hearts towards God are blinded in ignorance and unable to see or accept the truth of the Gospel. They count the Gospel as foolishness. The unbeliever is alienated and darkened from the truth of scripture, unable to see the light of the Gospel that reveals Jesus Christ as Lord and Savior.

Only when your heart starts to soften towards God do you begin your spiritual awakening. Your spiritual awakening leads to the beginning of understanding scripture and your journey towards eternal salvation through Jesus Christ. The God of this world is a direct reference to Satan.

We have a very different story through the lens of believers, bringing us to our third moral of the above narrative, which is:

(Romans 10:10)
"So then faith comes by hearing, and hearing by the word of God."

(Psalm 119:105)
"Your word is a lamp for my feet, a light on my path."

(Colossians 2:2)
"My goal is that they may be encouraged in heart and united in love, so that they may have the full riches of complete understanding, in order that they may know the mystery of God, namely, Christ,"

Faith is a product of belief. Once you believe in the Lord Jesus Christ and have accepted Him as your Lord and Savior, you become what we call "Born

Again" and sanctified. If you have true belief in your heart and not just a shallow confession with your mouth, you are on the road to true faith and sanctification. Once you are saved and begin to absorb the Word of God, you experience incredible growth and start to mature in your faith. You begin to exhibit what is called the fruit of the spirit and produce good works.

(Galatians 5:22-23)
"But the fruit of the Spirit is love, joy, peace, forbearance, kindness, goodness, faithfulness, gentleness and self-control. Against such things there is no law."

(Ephesians 2:9-10)
"not by works so that no one can boast. For we are God's handiwork, created in Christ Jesus to do good works, which God prepared in advance for us to do."

Please keep in mind. You cannot work your way into salvation lest any man boast. Salvation is a free gift of grace from God. No amount of goodness or good works gives you a free pass. The indication is, once saved, your saving faith should produce good works.

God's word begins to light your path and illuminate your understanding of Him and his Word. Belief is the starting point of the Christians' walk with God. Without belief, there can be no faith or understanding. Good works alone do not produce salvation.

What is this "Born Again" term? The term comes from John 3:3-5. A Jewish Pharisee by the name of Nicodemus did not understand the term "Born Again." This is the explanation Jesus gave him:

(John 3:3-5)
"Jesus answered him, "I assure you and most solemnly say to you, unless a person is born again [reborn from above— spiritually transformed, renewed, sanctified], he cannot [ever] see and experience the kingdom of God." Nicodemus said to Him, "How can a man be born when he is old? He cannot enter his mother's womb a second time and be born, can he?" Jesus answered, "I assure you and most solemnly say to you, unless one is born of water and the Spirit he cannot [ever] enter the Kingdom of God. (AMP)"

You might have heard the term "Babes in Christ." This term refers to the new believer. It signifies that new believers in Christ are like babies. We are not talking about literal babies, but it is an analogy that describes the needs of an infant in Christ, the new believer, to the needs of a newborn infant. They are similar in scope and intensity.

What does a newborn infant require? Love, nurturing, food, clothing, shelter, instruction, companionship, and correction. When all these are present, the infant matures into a healthy, functioning adult ready to participate in society. When some of these elements are missing in a child's life, trouble arises.

The new Christian or "Babe in Christ" requires all these elements to grow, mature, or develop in faith in their young walk. When all or some of these items are missing, the new Christian falters. The Body of Christ and His church is tasked with guiding the teaching and growth of the new believer. A task that today is neglected in most churches. The majority of churches today have become theatres of entertainment rather than houses of God for His worship, fellowship, prayer, discipleship, correction, and sound Biblical teaching.

(1 Peter 2:22)
"like newborn babies [you should] long for the pure milk of the word, so that by it you may be nurtured and grow in respect to salvation [its ultimate fulfillment]," (AMP)

Once again, I hear you saying. "This is all great, Brian, and sounds like some of the basic tenets of Christianity and salvation. However, what does all that have to do with reading, interpreting, and learning my Bible, which I thought this book was about?" Again, everything. We are building the foundation to understanding.

If you are not a true believer in your heart and do not know Christ as described above, the Bible will mean nothing to you, as indicated by the Bible itself. It will be mumble jumbo. You will walk away scoffing and mocking the truth of the word. You must be a Born Again true believer in Jesus Christ for the scriptures to have true meaning and to have that meaning and knowledge revealed to you. Without true salvation, you will never be able to unravel the truth and mystery of the Word. It is the starting point.

If you do not yet know the saving grace of Jesus Christ and the salvation He offers, in other words, you are not yet saved or are not yet a Born Again

Christian, don't despair yet. Or, if you are a poser and faking Christ or have been deceived into a false salvation, which you are probably unaware of, don't despair yet.

The discourse above has not been written to discourage you from reading the Bible. Reading the Bible is one of the beginning roads to salvation. Read the Bible! Reading the Bible and hearing the Word of God is the gateway to the true faith, as Romans 10:17 tells us.

(Romans 10:17)
"So faith comes from hearing [what is told], and what is heard comes by the [preaching of the] message concerning Christ."
(AMP)

I am pointing out that true understanding and proper interpretation will not be revealed to you until you have true faith and salvation as indicated by the scriptures. Your heart is darkened beyond true understanding and comprehension. I didn't say it. God did in His Word many times. Yup, I am aware this is a harsh reality, but nonetheless, it is a scriptural truth and fact, as we have quoted in a number of the above verses.

Up to this point, we have been building the foundation to move us forward into how we read, interpret and understand God's word. The foundation is set. The next step is to dig right in. We have been relying so far on the actual Word of God to lead us to where we are. You might have noticed that we have not used any supplemental works or writings to get us here. This has been intentional.

Supplemental works, videos, or books by Godly authors can help you in your study and have value, as can preaching and teaching from the pulpit, home study groups and Godly mentors. However, all those items or activities are, or should be, based on the Word of God and secondary in support of your scripture study and reading. So for our purpose, we are only going directly to the source, God's Word. God tells us that each of us who are his children can read and understand His Word, the Bible.

(Psalm 119:30)
"The unfolding of your words gives light;
it gives understanding to the simple."

(Proverbs 2:6)
"For the Lord gives wisdom;
from his mouth come knowledge and understanding."

(2 Corinthians 1:12-13)

"Now this is our boast: Our conscience testifies that we have conducted ourselves in the world, and especially in our relations with you, with integrity and godly sincerity. We have done so, relying not on worldly wisdom but on God's grace. For we do not write you anything you cannot read or understand."

As we unfold or read and study God's Word, we begin to gain understanding. From God's mouth comes His Word, resulting in knowledge and understanding when we absorb it through reading, prayer, and meditation. According to 2 Corinthians 1:12-13, nothing has been written that we cannot understand. Scripture is pretty clear and straightforward. It has been written for our consumption and understanding. So let's dig in and see how all this understanding comes about, starting with how to read the Word.

Chapter Four
HOW SHOULD I READ THE BIBLE?

There are some essential prerequisites when you begin to sit down to read and study the Bible to get the most out of each session. The first one is prayer. When we study God's Word seeking wisdom and understanding, these come directly from God. When we prayerfully consider the Word, God reveals the mystery of the Gospel to us, and we are blessed because of it. The scriptures are full of admonitions and instructions to pray.

The scriptures are also full of Godly men praying through the Word. When we read scripture, we should pause frequently and ask God for the wisdom, understanding, revelation, and application of the verses under consideration. We should then pray through the scripture. As an example, when we read in Philippians 2:14-16.

(Philippians 2:14-16)
"Do everything without grumbling or arguing, so that you may become blameless and pure, "children of God without fault in a warped and crooked generation." Then you will shine among them like stars in the sky as you hold firmly to the word of life.

And then I will be able to boast on the day of Christ that I did not run or labor in vain."

How do we pray through the scripture? First, read the verse a couple of times and meditate on the words and meaning. (I cover meditation in a second.) Read the verse out loud. Think of how the verse applies to your life or actions and what God's expectation is for you. Why did He write this verse for you to consume? What does God have for you, and how do you apply it to your life. In what context was it written. (More on context in a bit). Meditate on these thoughts. Ask the Holy Spirit for wisdom and understanding to help you unravel the meaning and application of what you are reading.

A whole sermon could be written about these two verses. There is a lot here. Once you are comfortable that you understand the meaning and purpose of what God has written for you, commit the verse to prayer and maybe memory if you are capable. I do have a complete chapter later on teaching you how to memorize God's Word effectively. Once ready, bow in prayer. It might look like this:

"Father, I bow in prayer to recognize your Holiness before you and give you all praises and account to you all glory and power. Hallowed be your name. Lord, may your will be done. As I read this verse in Philippians, I count my blessings that you have written it for my instruction. Help me to write your Word of life within my heart and mind. Lord, help me to walk blameless and pure before you in Christ. Please help me purge all grumbling and arguing from my life that I might shine like a light on a hill to this warped and crooked generation. May they come to know you through my living your example. My deep desire is to labour for your glory and to be counted worthy on the day of your return. In your precious name, may your Kingdom come. Amen."

When you read and pray through God's Word, you will mature and grow as a Christian and draw near to God day by day. You will mature in Christ and in your walk with Him. What a blessing God has given us to know and love His Word.

We are not talking about rambling off some pre-written prayer or mantra from our intellect in some repetitive fashion devoid of meaning or emotion. We are talking about heartfelt, spirit lead prayer to God your Creator, over the scripture you are reading, with thanksgiving and humble supplication before Him.

In Ephesians 6:18-20, Paul instructs us to pray in the spirit on all occasions with all kinds of prayers and requests. Reading scripture certainly qualifies as an occasion.

(Ephesians 6:18-20)
"And pray in the Spirit on all occasions with all kinds of prayers and requests. With this in mind, be alert and always keep on praying for all the Lord's people. Pray also for me, that whenever I speak, words may be given me so that I will fearlessly make known the mystery of the gospel, for which I am an ambassador in chains. Pray that I may declare it fearlessly, as I should."

Another fundamental concept when studying the Word is meditation. The first thing that might come to your mind is some occult, Eastern mysticism, transcendental meditation, or Yoga, things we are to have nothing to do with or a bunch of guys in robes on some mountain in Tibet. This is not what I am inferring. The scriptures are full of Biblical examples of meditation. Again, we will point to the scriptures for our examples. Throughout scripture, we are admonished to meditate on God, the works of His hands and accomplishments in our lives and the world, on His Word, and what is yet to come. It is a fundamental concept to help us grow in our faith and the understanding of God.

When we blow through the reading of scripture without giving it any thought or seeking its understanding and application, we do ourselves a disservice. What does it mean to meditate on God's Word? The Merriam-Webster Dictionary defines meditation as such:

1: to engage in contemplation or reflection
2: to engage in mental exercise for the purpose of reaching a heightened level of spiritual awareness

Merriam-Webster got it wrong, which should come as no surprise being a publication of the world. The Bible gives us a more profound and proper meaning of what Biblical meditation is. In the very first Psalm in the first two verses, David sets the stage for when we should meditate on the scriptures. All-day long, and all night long. That translates to always!

(Psalm 1:1-2)
"Blessed is the one who does not walk in step with the wicked or stand in the way that sinners take or sit in the company of mockers, but whose delight is in the law of the Lord, and who meditates on his law day and night."

Also, Both Asaph in Psalm 77:11-12 and David in Psalm 143:5 describe meditation as a three-step process. We are to remember, ponder and then meditate.

(Psalm 143:5)
"I remember the days of long ago;
I meditate on all your works
and consider (ponder) what your hands have done."

You will notice that these examples of meditation focus on God, His law, and His Word, not us. We are to remember what He has accomplished, ponder or consider the works of His hands, and then reflect or meditate, meaning to think deeply on these things. Biblical meditation is not self-reflection. It is a reflection on God and his works, law and Word. In Philippians 4:8, we are given an even deeper look at Biblical meditation.

(Philippians 4:8)
"Finally, brethren, whatever things are true, whatever things are noble, whatever things are just, whatever things are pure, whatever things are lovely, whatever things are of good report, if there is any virtue and if there is anything praiseworthy—meditate on these things." (NKJV)

This passage admonishes us to take from the scriptures all that is true, noble, just, pure, lovely, of good report, virtuous and praiseworthy, and meditate on these attributes of God and His word before Him. We see Him in all his infinite wisdom and glory when we steep our hearts and minds on God and his Word in quiet God-centered meditation.

Meditation helps us draw near to God, renew our spirit, and gain victory over what is impure and of bad report in our lives. It helps us to draw closer to God. Meditation also gives us a deeper understanding of what God has for each of us. The concept of meditation, pondering, and contemplation can be found over 100 times between the Old and New Testaments. It is an essential and critical part of our daily worship.

Once we incorporate prayer and meditation into our daily study, the next area to help us understand how to read the Bible is the structure of the Bible. The 66 Bible books are divided into sections and subsections by the compilers by types of books and authors. Understanding what type of book you are reading is paramount for understanding and interpretation. For example, you will interpret a book of prophecy very differently from a book of history or wisdom.

Thinking about how you organize information on your computer will help you understand how the Bible is arranged. If you are like most people, you will create folders to store your information. These folders will typically be named by the type of information you are storing. You might have made folders for pictures, emails, recipes, bills, and so on. When you classify each piece of information you are dealing with, you will store it in its respective folder—bills to the bill folder, emails to the email folder, and onward. The Bible follows this exact same pattern.

The first major division in the Bible is between the Old and New Testaments. As I have pointed out, there are 39 Old Testament Books followed by 27 New Testament books. This one is easy. All the Old Testament Books were written before the Birth of Jesus and cover the patriarchs, the Law, prophecy, the coming Messiah, Isreal, and what is to come. The New Testament books were all written after the birth of Jesus and focus on His ministry, the Church Age, salvation, grace and what is to come. It is essential to know that the Old Testament points to, through narrative and prophecies, the coming of the Messiah,

Jesus. The New Testament covers the fulfilment of the Old Testament prophecies about Jesus. Old Testament prophecies are referenced throughout the New Testament. The entirety of the Bible is Christ-centered.

The Old Testament is broken down into five categories of books in order:

5 Books of the Law: Genesis, Exodus, Leviticus, Numbers, and Deuteronomy.

12 Books of History: Joshua, Judges, Ruth, 1 Samuel, 2 Samuel, 1 Kings, 2 Kings, 1 Chronicles, 2 Chronicles, Ezra, Nehemiah, and Esther.

5 Books of wisdom: Job, Psalms, Proverbs, Ecclesiastes, and the Song of Solomon.

17 Books of Prophecy, 5 Major Prophets and 12 Minor Prophets: Major - Isaiah, Jeremiah, Lamentations, Ezekiel, Daniel, Minor - Hosea, Joel, Amos, Obadiah, Jonah, Micah, Nahum, Habakkuk, Zephaniah, Haggai, Zechariah, and Malachi.

The New Testament is broken down into four categories of books in order:

4 Gospels: Matthew, Mark, Luke, and John.

1 Book of History: Acts

21 Epistles: Romans, 1 Corinthians, 2 Corinthians, Galatians, Ephesians, Philippians, Colossians, 1 Thessalonians, 2 Thessalonians, 1 Timothy, 2 Timothy, Titus, Philemon, Hebrews, James, 1 Peter, 2 Peter, 1 John, 2 John, 3 John, and Jude.

1 Apocalyptic Book: Revelation.

The Old Testament

5 Books of the Law

The first five books of the Bible tell the story of the creation of the heavens and earth, mankind and the establishment of the Nation of Isreal and the law. We are introduced to our Triune God, His adversary, the Devil, original sin, and the fall of man. We are also introduced to many of the famous Old Testament characters and well-known stories like the flood and Jonah, with Moses emerging as one of the central figures. One of the main themes throughout these books is redemption. Recounting Israel's escape and salvation from Egypt, the narrative tells the story of Israel's continuing cycle of disobedience, consequences, repentance, and blessings. Threaded throughout these five books are the genealogies leading from Adam to David, pointing to the coming Messiah.

The law is a series of commands and instructions to the people of Isreal. We are introduced to Ceremonial Law dealing with and managing the temple, tabernacle, the sacrificial system, implements of sacrifice, types of acceptable sacrifices, the Arc of the covenant, ceremonies, festivals, and religious affairs administered by the tribe of Levi. We also find Civil Law overseen by appointed Judges and representatives and Moral law applicable to all people of the Isreal Nation.

The five books of Moses are also historical narratives recounting actual events that happened to real people through this initial time of our history. These books should be read in a literal sense allowing for a spattering of symbolism and imagery.

13 Books of History
The historical books retell the factual events of history from Adam onwards throughout to Christ in

both the Old and New Testament times. They tell the story of what happened to who and when framed by God's faithfulness and redemptive work for mankind. Over 40% of the scriptures are historical narratives giving us a clear picture of what has come before us. A literal reading and interpretation with a straightforward approach are how you should read Historical books.

5 Books of Wisdom

The five books of wisdom are broken down into two categories. Psalms and Song of Solomon are considered poetic in nature with elements of songs, poems, prayers and worship. In this type of literary scripture, you will encounter figurative language, symbolism, pictures in words, metaphors and parallel synonyms. They are full of the expression of emotion and love for God. David, one of the prominent authors of Psalms, devotes some of his writing to beseeching God's hand for protection from enemies and relief from his distresses. Some of the best-known and loved verses in the Bible come from poetic books. You will find some elements of poetic literature throughout the Bible. You read poetic literature with the understanding you will encounter verses that require interpretation. We look at interpretation in the next chapter.

The Song of Solomon is a poetic set of lyrical dialogues of poems written by a woman to her lover with occasional input from a chorales third party. The ESV Study Bible breaks the Psalms into the following categories.

- Laments (laying a troubled situation before the Lord and asking for help)

- Hymns of thanksgiving, praise, the celebration of God's law, and prophecy.

- Psalms of wisdom, confidence, history and royalty (dealing with the Davidic monarchy and the coming Messiah)

The second category of wisdom literature is just that, wisdom literature. The books of Job, Ecclesiastes, and Proverbs are considered wisdom literature. Solomon, deemed the wisest man ever to walk this earth, is credited with writing Ecclesiastes, most Proverbs, and Lamentations.

Job and Ecclesiastes are narrative in scope and reflective works on the toils of life and struggles with the evil one, pointing to trust in God and His redemptive work. Proverbs is a collection of 31 chapters of wise sayings profitable for ethical and wise living before God, including morality, proper behaviours and speech. Each Proverb is a set of two poetic lines long. The first line is an action, good or bad, and the second line is the reward or consequence of the above line's action.

It is best to read these books with the knowledge that they are full of profound, Biblical truths and principles that you will mine and extract through clear thought and reflection as you go through their narratives. You read them with more of a literal poetic sense. You seek to apply the wisdom they teach to your own words and actions in life to avoid the pitfalls and embrace the activities of the wisdom they teach.

17 Books of Prophecy

A Prophet in the Old Testament is an individual anointed by God to deliver God's message to the people. The message to be delivered was divine revelation from God. A prophecy was given to the people through the Prophets in many ways. Sometimes it was plain language. Other times it was fanciful visions, dreams, symbolism, metaphors or imagery. In other times it was through a physical event, symbolic gesture or practice. The Biblical test of a true Prophet is if the prophecy came or comes true, past, present or future. The Bible also warns many times about following false prophets. A false prophet is someone who claims they have a divine, personal or unique revelation from God but do not, and their prophecy does not come true.

(Matthew 7:15) "Beware of false prophets, who come to you in sheep's clothing, but inwardly they are ravenous wolves." (NKJV)

The prophetic books of scripture are the most difficult to understand and interpret because of their literary style and content. Most Christians shy away from these books but should not. Only when the entirety of the Bible is read and understood can we see God's plan and its unfolding.

One of the central themes the Prophets dealt with was the nation of Israel's rejection and betrayal of God's laws, idol worship, their sin and their turning away from God and his resulting judgement. The Prophets delivered clear messages of consequence, exile, and separation from God if they continued in sin and rebellion, or reward and blessing if they returned to God and his laws. These consequences varied from separation from God, being stripped of their land and possessions, exile from the land, defeat in battle, famines, droughts and plagues, and the list goes on. Repentance and returning to follow God and his laws were rewarded mercy, restoration, forgiveness, abundance and blessing.

One of the other central themes of prophecy is the coming Messiah and His Kingdom. Most Christians assume the majority of Old Testament prophecy concerns the coming Messiah. They do not. Less than 5% of the Old Testament prophecies concern Jesus and the New Covenant. The majority of these prophecies concern the plight of the nation of Isreal.

There are a number of steps you can take to help you interpret Biblical prophecies.

You need to take into account the historical time, culture, and context the Prophets were writing. The figures of speech and nuances of language and culture were much different than our modern-day speech and culture. Consulting historical writings, commentaries, lexicons, and the scriptures themselves will help in this area. Interpreting prophecy will take some prayerful time and effort led by the Holy Spirit. You should not become discouraged when reading and seeking to understand prophecy. Time and effort will reward you

You need to understand and learn what some of the prophetic imagery, symbols and objects represent.

Knowing what is represented by a presented symbol or object goes a long way in interpreting language, intent and meaning. For example, a dove represents Holiness, innocence, and purity and often represents the Holy Spirit in scripture. The Prophets use a multitude of symbols and objects in their writings. There are many good books written solely on the topic of Biblical imagery and objects. It would be beneficial to invest in one of these books to aid you in your study. It would take the entirety of this book to cover and explain the meaning of all the symbols and imagery in the scriptures.

Knowing what numbers represent in the Bible is also an essential aspect of understanding the Bible, Biblical prophecy, and the Prophets' writing. Again, this is a topic that would need many books to explore fully. The mathematical laws God has designed and put in place speak volumes to his magnificent glory, power and point to the only possibility of our existence as created beings. For our purpose, I will state that knowing the significance and meaning of at least specific numbers will help us with Biblical interpretation.

The number 40, for example, denotes a period of testing, trial, or discipline. When you read the scriptures and come across an instance of the number

40, you would know that one of the above circumstances is taking place. You can find over 150 references or examples of this number in use. Each number in the scriptures has both a spiritual and practical significance. The number 7 is referenced over 860 times in the scriptures.

God punished Isreal by making them wander 40 years in the desert before bringing them into the promised land. The Prophet Jonah warned Nineva for 40 days and 40 nights of their coming destruction if they did not repent and turn to God. Elija went 40 days without food and water, Jesus was tempted by Satan 40 days and 40 nights in the desert, Isreal was sent into exile 40 years after the crucifixion. The list goes on and on. You gain insight into how to contextualize and interpret scriptures surrounding and including the number 40 as one example.

As with symbols, objects and imagery, there are many excellent books dedicated to studying numbers in the Bible. I would encourage you to pick a good one up and add it to your study reference library. Studying what numbers represent and their use throughout scripture will tremendously aid you in your growth and understanding of the Bible and what God is conveying to you through His written Word.

You will always want to look for scripture interpreting scripture. What I mean when I say that is you will encounter a prophecy that appears cryptic and challenging to understand. A good example would be Nebuchadnezzar's dream in Daniel 2. In this chapter, Nebuchadnezzer's magicians, enchanters, sorcerers, and astrologers could not interpret his dream. The King has Daniel summoned to give an account of its meaning.

Daniel interprets the dream by describing a statue of varying values of precious metals from the head decreasing in value as you move towards the feet and ending in ten toes of iron and clay. Then Daniel goes on to describe the destruction of that statue. If you were to stop reading there, you would be left in confusion.

Fortunately, Daniel interprets the dreams meaning and describes 4 Kingdoms starting with Nebuchadnezzar's Kingdom represented by the head of gold and its destruction. Ultimately, the successive three kingdoms to rise and fall are represented by the dream. This interpretation was a prophetic revelation of what was to come. Except for the final Kingdom that we await, this prophecy has been fulfilled through time precisely as given. The interpretation ends with the setting up of God's final Kingdom, the 5th and final Kingdom, that will endure throughout eternity.

Another good example is at the beginning of chapter 1 of Revelation. When John was in the Spirit on the Lord's day, he heard a loud voice behind him like the sound of a trumpet. When he looked behind him, he saw seven golden lampstands, and among them, he saw someone dressed like the Son of man. Coming out of his mouth was a sharp double-edged sword, and in his right hand, he held seven stars.

My goodness, that all sounds so cryptic. How can one ever understand its meaning? The good news is it's straightforward. We simply have to read on a little and reference a couple of other areas of scripture. If we read on through to verse 20, scripture interprets scripture. It tells us straight out that the seven lampstands represent the seven churches and the seven stars represent the angels of the seven churches. We also know from other passages of scripture that the sharp double-edged sword represents the word of God, and the Son of man represents Jesus. How easy was that?

There are many instances of scripture interpreting scripture. Sometimes you will find prophetic interpretation directly after the prophecy. At other times it will be further on in the book or even in another book of the Bible. This model extends right into the New Testament. Often, New Testament text refers to Old Testament prophecies or teaching and gives the true meaning of what was inferred but misunderstood or unknown when written.

Prophecy is one of the many wonders and mysteries of God's Word for us to unravel. There is nothing more exciting to see God's prophetic Word fulfilled throughout history. What was, what is and what is to come. Absorbing yourself in prophecy and unravelling the mysteries it offers can be one of the most rewarding pursuits you will ever undertake. With prayer, the Holy Spirits' guidance, studying the Word, getting some assistance from secondary resources and a desire to write God's word in your heart and mind, you can learn and know prophecy.

The New Testament

4 Gospels

The first four books of the New Testament are called the Gospels. The word gospel means "Good News." Each of the four Gospels recounts the birth, life, ministry, crucifixion and resurrection of Jesus from a unique perspective. The Gospels are theological, historical narratives. Many have wondered through the ages why we need four gospels. Would not one be sufficient? I believe there are many reasons God has seen fit to include the four distinct but parallel Gospel Books.

Firstly, John gives us a glimpse. One of the reasons we find directly in his Gospel.

(John 21:25) "And there are also many other things that Jesus did, which if they were written one by one, I suppose that even the world itself could not contain the books that would be written. Amen." (NKJV)

Each of the Gospel authors came from different backgrounds and levels of education. Matthew was a tax collector. Mark was a writer and a scribe. Luke was a physician. John was a fisherman. They each wrote from their unique perspective and highlighted different aspects of the life and ministry of Jesus.

Matthew focused on bridging the narrative between the Old and New Testaments for the Jew and makes frequent references to the Law and Prophecy. He focuses on the role of Jesus as the coming Messiah and that he fulfills the Old Testament messianic prophecies about the saviour and coming King. He includes the genealogy to show that Jesus is of the root, or the seed, of David.

The Gospel of Mark is an arranged essay of Peter's ministry and memoirs through time and written for a broad audience. It is less concerned with recording the sermons of Jesus that the other Gospels recount and more concerned with action. Mark's Gospel clearly spells out that Christianity is not a spectator sport. It is a Gospel with a call to action. One of the main themes within this Gospel is to repent and believe, the Kingdom of God is at hand.

The Gospel of Luke is the longest book in the New Testament and displays an educated man's writing skill and style, which makes sense given his profession as a doctor. Lukes Gospel focuses on Jesus's ministry to the downcast and outcast with an emphasis on Jesus as the saviour of all mankind. It is written in chronological order and resembles a journalistic book of history and learning. Luke was the only non-Hebrew author in the scriptures.

The Gospel of John focuses strongly on Jesus's miracles and signs, focusing on the divine nature of Jesus. He seeks to walk the reader through coming to believe in Jesus for salvation and everlasting life. John goes into the deepest details describing our struggle with the evil one, our adversary, the Devil, and his minions. John emphasizes the power of Jesus to ultimately destroy Satan's workings and achieve victory over evil. John is a pervasive Gospel and one of the best starting points for a new Christian or for those seeking to learn about the saving grace of Jesus Christ.

The Gospels are historical narratives of actual events involving actual people and should be read as such. Within them, you will find imagery, symbolism, parallelisms, metaphors and parables. More often than not, the interpretation of the symbolism and imagery is given right within the Gospels themselves or within the 21 epistles that follow the book of Acts.

Parables found within the Gospels are narrated stories to teach a Biblical truth or spiritual lesson regarding Holy living, morality, action, or speech. Jesus explains a number of the parables within the writings of the Gospels. Many Christians, including even some Pastors, make the mistake of teaching that the parables were actual events involving real people. They are not. When reading the parables within the Gospels, you will want to seek out what message and teaching Jesus portrays to you through the story and how to apply that message to your life.

1 Book of History

The book of Acts, written by Luke, is a book of history that chronicles and expounds on the early church's establishment, development, growth, and ministry. It covers the early church from the ascension of Jesus through to its time of writing, estimated to be between 70 and 80 A.D. The central characters are Peter and Paul. Because the book of Acts is a book of history, you read it in a literal sense. The characters in the story are actual people and narrates the happenings in the first century time period.

21 Epistles

Paul wrote the first 13 Epistles, Romans through to Philemon. Pauls Epistles were either addressed to a specific individual or spiritual instructions to the church he was communicating with on faith, love, hope, and morality. They often included a component of correction. The Epistles were also authoritative. Paul's Epistles were also either a letter of introduction or preparation for a visit he was planning. The balance of the 8 Epistles were generally written to a larger audience or region. Their teaching keeps in line with what we read from Paul.

All 21 Epistles are in some shape or form letters of instruction and or requests, as is the case with

Philemon. They are historical in nature, and you should read them in a literal sense. You will find some imagery and symbolism within the letters; however, the imagery and symbolism are straightforward and often available elsewhere in the scriptures for interpretation when encountered.

1 Book of Revelation

The book of Revelation is an apocalyptic book that reveals divine mysteries of what is to come, an unveiling of something yet unknown. It is an essential book to understand what is at hand and coming in these end times. Time and effort should be spent in this book to understand what is to come soon. Sadly, many Pastors, Christians, and churches avoid the book of Revelation.

The first three chapters are predominantly letters of chastising and instruction to the seven churches in the province of Asia. From chapter 4 onward, the church is never mentioned again. The balance of the book deals with God's coming judgements in what we know as the coming 7-year tribulation, the defeat of the antichrist and Satan, and the ultimate setting up of the Kingdom of God with Christ as the future King.

The book of Revelation is steeped in symbolism and imagery. To understand this book, you will need to prayerfully consider the teachings of the Prophets, of Jesus, and have a good knowledge of the Epistles. The interpretation of the book of revelation is the most contested book in the Bible. Many will lead you astray with their interpretation of this book. I don't believe anyone, past or present, has a complete grasp on all that's been revealed. As time marches onward and we get closer to the events of the book, more of its mystery is being revealed. We can now see how some of its prophecies will come about with globalization afoot, technology abounding, and the nations aligning to surrender their leadership to the antichrist just as the populations are now surrendering their freedoms to government overreach.

Your best bet is to take the book slowly, consult good commentaries, dictionaries, lexicons, and books on symbolism and imagery. Most importantly, test everything you read against scripture and be cautious about being led down the rabbit hole with this one. Spending time in this book and reading it aloud will bring you a special blessing and wisdom in Christ. We are admonished to read it and take to heart what is written in it.

(Revelation 1:3)
"Blessed is the one who reads aloud the words of this prophecy, and blessed are those who hear it and take to heart what is written in it, because the time is near."

The purpose of this chapter has been to help bring clarity and understanding to what the Bible is. Simplistic in form, and by God's Divinity brought together in a collection of books to tell a story. The story of the unfailing love our Creator has for his creation, you and me. The story of how God desires a loving relationship with us and how we can have one with him through eternal salvation in Christ, his Son. God saves us by His grace alone, not by works lest any man boast.

(Ephesians 2:9)
"not as a result of [your] works [nor your attempts to keep the Law], so that no one will [be able to] boast or take credit in any way [for his salvation]." (AMP)

Throughout these assembled books, he tells us of our history, what we have in Him today, and what the future holds for all mankind – both saved and lost. (Spoiler alert. The story's ending is not good for those who do not know him, the lost.) One of the central themes of the Bible is the assembled story of relationships with God and with one another. Once we have salvation in Christ, the expectation is that we will mature in our faith and produce good works through this process. Not a saving works but good works as a result of our salvation.

(James 2:14-17)
"What does it profit, my brethren, if someone says he has faith but does not have works? Can faith save him? If a brother or sister is naked and destitute of daily food, and one of you says to them, "Depart in peace, be warmed and filled," but you do not give them the things which are needed for the body, what does it profit? Thus also faith by itself, if it does not have works, is dead…" (NKJV)

Here is where the first problem arises. How can one achieve maturity in faith, produce good works, be obedient to the Word, and develop a relationship with God and each other according to the teaching of scripture if we never read or absorb ourselves in it? The majority of those claiming Christ do not read their Bible daily or even monthly. We are to be doers of the Word. How can you do what you do not know?

(James 1:22)
"Do not merely listen to the word, and so deceive yourselves. Do what it says."

To be a doer of the Word, we need to be absorbed in the Word. If we listen but do not do, we are deceiving ourselves, and the truth is not in us. James goes on to say that by absorbing ourselves in the Word and abiding by it, we will be blessed and favored by God because of it.

(James 1: 25)
"But he who looks carefully into the perfect law, the law of liberty, and faithfully abides by it, not having become a [careless] listener who forgets but an active doer [who obeys], he will be blessed and favored by God in what he does [in his life of obedience]." (AMP)

And that is the second admonition of this chapter. To encourage you to be in the word daily in prayerful study and meditation. To learn the blueprint God has designed for your life and to draw near to him daily. You will be strengthened and comforted in Him as you achieve peace and well-being.

(Philippians 4:9-11)
"The things which you have learned and received and heard and seen in me, practice these things [in daily life], and the God [who is the source] of peace and well-being will be with you." (AMP)

And this brings us to the most vocalized stumbling block. I hear time and time again, "Brian, I just don't understand it." There are reasons for this that you can overcome. As we briefly touched on earlier, one of the major stumbling blocks in today's liberal, compromising, failing church is false teaching and preaching. In many places, a Gospel is taught that you do not find in the scriptures. One that has been perverted in meaning and truth.

Where the confusion gets worse, in addition to a false Gospel, each of these heretics promotes their own distorted version leaving you to sift through conflicting false teaching. How do you discern false Gospel teaching? Know the true Gospel and how to interpret the Word. This is where our next chapter leads us, how do we interpret the Word of God correctly handling its truths.

(2 Timothy 2:15)
"Be diligent to present yourself approved to God, a worker who does not need to be ashamed, rightly dividing the word of truth."

Chapter Five
HOW TO INTERPRET THE BIBLE

This chapter will look at how not to read the Bible, as our book title indicates. How have we ended up with seemingly dedicated, devoted Bible teachers and preachers all teaching a conflicting message regarding Bible interpretation and theology? How does the church of Christ continue to splinter and divide, creating offshoot after offshoot of denominations in opposition to one another?

How is it that the majority of the internet Christian warriors spend the bulk of their time attacking one another and everyone else and their uncle over doctrine and theology? How have cults continued to thrive and grow? How have we ended up with our churches full of spiritually dead people? People who, maybe, show up to church once a week to check a box and then continue their lives as usual with no evidence of any spiritual fruit in their lives or a Christian walk?

The current state of affairs within the church and the majority of those who claim Christ is disappointing, bewildering, and just plain sad to see and watch. The world is watching and laughing. One of the commissions to the Christian is to walk in the light and be a light in this dark world and set a Godly example in speech, actions and deeds so that they may see Christ through and in you unto their salvation. Light symbolizes God, faith and Holiness through scripture.

It appears the church has become a mockery and pushes more people away than it attracts with its failings both internally and externally. We see this in the continuing national decline in those claiming Christ or attending church. The church and those in it appear to be walking in darkness. It should not be this way, but it is. Why?

(1 John 1:5-9)
"This is the message we have heard from him and declare to you: God is light; in him there is no darkness at all. If we claim to have fellowship with him and yet walk in the darkness, we lie and do not live out the truth. But if we walk in the light, as he is in the light, we have fellowship with one another, and the blood of Jesus, his Son, purifies us from all sin."

(Matthew 5:16)
"In the same way, let your light shine before others, that they may see your good deeds and glorify your Father in heaven."

I am not suggesting that we should never call out false teaching. Of course, we should, and the Bible indicates this in multiple verses. Jesus spent a lot of his time calling out and warning about false prophets, teachers and doctrine, as did the majority of the New Testament authors. I am also not suggesting that every church, teacher and preacher is leading people astray. There remains a remnant of sound preaching, pastors, teachers and churches out there. The question is, how do you discern the good from the bad, the Godly from the ungodly?

(1 Timothy 6:3-5)
If anyone teaches a different doctrine and does not agree with the sound words of our Lord Jesus Christ and the teaching that accords with godliness, he is puffed up with conceit and understands nothing. He has an unhealthy craving for controversy and for quarrels about words, which produce envy, dissension, slander, evil suspicions, and constant friction among people who are depraved in mind and deprived of the truth, imagining that godliness is a means of gain. (ESV)

(Romans 16:17-18)
I appeal to you, brothers, to watch out for those who cause divisions and create obstacles contrary to the doctrine that you have been taught; avoid them. For such persons do not serve our

Lord Christ, but their own appetites, and by smooth talk and flattery they deceive the hearts of the naive. (ESV)

If we are all reading the same Bible or at least a similar translation, should we not all be on the same page with our theology and teaching the same message as we share Christ and the salvation message? One would think so. Unfortunately, scriptures teach us that there will be a falling away from sound doctrine and a departure from truth in these last days. Faithful Christians should not be surprised by what we see.

(1 Timothy 4:1)
"Now the Spirit expressly says that in later times some will depart from the faith by devoting themselves to deceitful spirits and teachings of demons," (ESV)

(2 Timothy 4:3-4)
"For the time is coming when people will not endure sound teaching, but having itching ears they will accumulate for themselves teachers to suit their own passions, and will turn away from listening to the truth and wander off into myths." (ESV)

These two verses indicate that teaching and preaching will be distorted and twisted to condone and excuse sinful lifestyles and behaviours in these last days. What was evil will be called good, and what is good will be called evil. The deceptions of the Devil drive this populous teaching and false doctrine driven by false teachers and preachers.

The mainstream church and a good portion of those claiming Christ have turned away from the true Gospel and are following deceiving spirits unto eternal separation from God. There is an ongoing and worsening abandonment of the truth of scripture. One day soon, we will see governments begin to suppress the true Bible message with laws and label those that preach the truth as uttering hate speech with the risk of imprisonment.

There are two main types of false teachers, preachers and evangelists. The first type is the outright heretic. These people preach a false Gospel and spew heresy for the purpose of self-enrichment. In other words, to get rich or to stoke an out-of-control ego and pride. Most of them are simply enriching themselves through theft and deception. Sure, they have learnt some popular Christian verses and throw them around to sound "Christiany," but the truth is not in them.

They are deceivers. These types of folks are not Christians. They are posers and pretenders. Although they pretend to be in Christ, he does not know them, and you should have nothing to do with them ever! Although they are not worth considering, we will set heretics aside for now and deal with them a little later. It is essential to have some framework to work with and know how to spot them and flee. We will deal with the second type of false teacher or preacher first.

Firstly, the second type of false teacher or preacher is the one who has a genuine desire to know and teach God's Word but has been led astray by seeking the truth of the word from other false teachers. The Bible admonishes us to test what is taught against the truth of scripture as we are taught in Acts 17:11.

(Acts 17:11)
"Now the Berean Jews were of more noble character than those in Thessalonica, for they received the message with great eagerness and examined the Scriptures every day to see if what Paul said was true."

Teachers need to do this, especially with their own teaching. Rather than mining and extracting the truth from scripture through prayerful consideration of the entirety of the word from beginning to end, the Bible has become secondary. The bulk of this teacher's time is spent reading and teaching what others teach who are caught up in the same trap. Their teaching becomes a circular discourse on falsehood, with each one of these teachers travelling around the same mary-go-round of error.

Secondly, this type of teacher adopts the currently favoured model of interpreting scripture as written allegorically. The method of allegorical interpretation supposes that the Bible has various levels of meaning, and the reader has the flexibility to interpret what it means to them. Personal interpretation is a grave error, and scripture speaks out against this practice.

(2 Peter 1:20)
"But understand this first of all, that no prophecy of Scripture is a matter of or comes from one's own [personal or special] interpretation," (AMP)

Some adopt a spiritual or mystical interpretation. For example, Lucifer, known as Satan, is not considered a real being but simply represents the struggle between good and evil. Although there is symbolism and imagery in the Bible, the interpretation of such items is not subjective to the reader's interpretative whim. Of course, this is a completely

misguided and incorrect view of Satan, an actual being
and our adversary who goes back and forth across this
earth looking for who he can devour.

Thirdly, this type of metaphorical pluralism has led
to views of pantheism, theosophical interpretation,
metaphysical interpretation, divine science and a
whole host of Bizzare teachings. These interpretations
have nothing to do with the scriptures. These views of
scripture promote the particular metaphysical or
religious system the interpreter adheres to rather than
the one static truth of the Word. By allegorizing
God's Word, people seek to justify and condone
immoral lifestyle choices and sin, presupposing
support from their misconstrued interpretation of the
scriptures, which is the furthest thing from the truth
of the Word.

In the current climate of social justice, and with the
victimization of truth and morality, bizarre
interpretations of the scriptures are adopted and
accepted. People now believe they have a right to
decide for themselves what a passage or verse means
to them rather than adhering to what the author
intended to say and convey. In other words, the truth
is in the eye of the beholder, so you can decide for
yourself what scriptural truth is to you. Those who

twist the words of scripture or misapply them are rebuked repeatedly in the Bible.

(2 Peter 3:16)
"Speaking about these things as he does in all of his letters. In which there are some things that are difficult to understand, which the untaught and unstable [who have fallen into error] twist and misinterpret, just as they do the rest of the Scriptures, to their own destruction." (AMP)

(Acts 13:10)
and said, "You son of the devil, you enemy of all righteousness, full of all deceit and villainy, will you not stop making crooked the straight paths of the Lord? (ESV)

The Bible is God's instruction and message to man written by men through divine inspiration from God. How we view God and his Word becomes distorted when we make the assumption and subsequent error of changing the Bible's literary intent. We should be very confident that God is capable and accurately relays his word to us through the Holy Scriptures for our understanding in clear speech and thought in a literal sense. It is crucial that we correctly interpret and handle God's Word to determine the Author's (God's) intended meaning in context rather than forcing our own ideas and misapplied theology into the text.

The alternative or allegorical interpretation of God's Word would make clear communication impossible and even futile. In this method of interpreting, the literal meaning is superficial, and the allegorical interpretation is considered accurate, albeit a changing truth to each individual based on their personal feelings of what the text says to them.

There would be no point in writing anything if the reader simply takes what they imagine from the verses and passages rather than take what the writer intended. Communication, both written and oral, is predicated on the presupposition that understood language conveys the author's clear intended meaning and communicated intention and instruction.

You do not have to look too far to figure out what is and has happened, to sound Biblical teaching and the continuing breakdown of society and its slide into moral decay. Replacing the absolute truth of scripture with a watered-down compromising version of varying falsehoods and compromises produces where we are today. The acceptance of allegorical Bible-teaching coupled with a population ready and willing to adopt the half-truths it produces has led us down the rabbit hole of a broken theology. Personal justification of immoral life choices and sin is the new normal and is now accepted in society rather than being rebuked by teachers of the Word.

So how do you not read the Bible as our book title asks? You should not allegorize the scriptures to justify your life choices or fit into a personal theology that contradicts the literal teaching of the Word. This methodology has nothing to do with the Bible and only produces a false Gospel. If you have to change or remove a single word of scripture to fit your interpretation of the text, your interpretation and theology are incorrect. You have made an error.

There is only one absolute truth within the Word of God. There is no subjectivity within the scriptures. We might not understand all of the symbolism and imagery we find in the Word, but these also have an absolute literal meaning or representation even if we have yet to figure it all out. If you do not understand a word, or a verse, or like what it says, you don't get to alter or delete it to fit your preference or theology. Your theology is misguided. If ten people interpret a scripture verse or passage in ten different ways, at least nine have gotten it wrong.

So how do we, with certainty, correctly handle the word of truth and the interpretation of God's Word? Although I have attempted to avoid most of the fanciful terms today's Bible teachers like to throw around to sound scholarly, there are a couple we will have to consider. When we seek to understand and interpret the scriptures, our singular goal is to understand what the authors intended to communicate to us and why.

To help us achieve the goal of interpretation and understanding, we have to prayerfully consider the historical setting of the time of writing, who wrote it, to whom the text is addressing, the text in context, and the type of book or passage we are reading. Is it historical, prophetic, wisdom, poetry, a Gospel or an Epistle? Our last bit of investigatory work is to seek a comparison of scripture with scripture of complementary or related writings.

Once we know as much information as we can about the text we are looking at, we need to consider three interpretation methodologies: Hermeneutics, Exegesis and Dispensation. Although this might all sound daunting, it is not. These are simple methods you use every day when you read and study any material to learn. We are simply attaching the accepted fancy terms to what you already know.

The word hermeneutics in its simplest form means the interpretation of language, written or oral. When applied to Biblical interpretation, its purpose is to bridge the gap between the minds of the Biblical writers at the time of writing and our own minds. We bridge this gap by having as much knowledge as possible about all of the items mentioned in the above paragraphs. We can define hermeneutics as the field of study that helps us with how we interpret the Bible.

In its simplest form, the word exegesis focuses on the word, grammar, and tense of the text or word. We use exegesis to analyze and draw out the meaning of the word or Biblical text. As you mature in your study and understanding of the Word, you will eventually begin to compare our modern translations of text and verses to the original languages.

The Bible was written in Hebrew, Greek and Aramaic. When studying the original languages, you will also consider the grammar, tense, and plurality of the words used. The study of the original languages is generally regarded as advanced study. Most new or young Christians will not go to this level when they initially seek to learn the scriptures.

Dispensationalism holds to a literal interpretation of the Bible as the best hermeneutics. The Dispensationalist breaks the scriptures into distinct periods of time or divinely appointed ages. For example, the Age of the Patriarchs – Adam to Abraham, the age of the Law – Abraham to Jesus, The age of grace – Jesus to His return, the Millennial Kingdom – Jesus 1000 year reign, Eternity with Christ on his eternal throne. Dispensationalism recognizes the uniqueness of the Church and the Nation of Isreal as two separate and distinct entities through the scripture narrative.

The Dispensationalist literal interpretation of scripture assigns each word in the Bible the meaning it would commonly have in everyday use at the time of writing. This same assignment is given to phrases, paragraphs, chapters and books. The Dispensationalist makes Allowances for symbolism, imagery, figures of speech and types. As mentioned previously, symbols, imagery, figures of speech and types have literal meanings behind them.

So, for one example, when the Bible speaks of "1000 Years" in the Book of Revelation chapter 20. The Dispensationalist interprets it as a literal period of 1000 years as we measure years. We would consider this 1000 years as described as the Dispensation of the Kingdom age. When there is no evidence of symbolism, imagery, or figures of speech, there is no compelling reason to interpret it otherwise. Dispensationalists accept the Books of Scripture contextually in 5 ways—books of History, Poetry/Wisdom, Prophecy, Gospels, and Epistles, as we looked at earlier.

When Jesus says at the beginning of *(John 10:9)*, *"I am the door."* The Dispensationalist understands that this is a symbolic image to which Jesus is referring. We do not assume Jesus is a literal door. You would never describe yourself as a door using literal language, as that would make no sense. Once we know we are dealing with symbolic speech, we seek to understand what is represented in the figurative or symbolic teaching.

Language has been given to us by God for the purpose of being able to communicate with one another effectively. Words are vessels with purpose and meaning. Philosophically, the purpose of language itself requires that we interpret words literally in order to be understood. Literalism is the best and only way to view the scriptures to understand what the authors intended to communicate to us.

When we attach allegorical subjectivity to the text, the original intent and meaning no longer exist. We are no longer interpreting scripture as intended. We are now interjecting our own authority into God's Word rather than submitting to His authority as given to us in the Biblical text. The crazy teachings we now see by the modern-day false preachers are good evidence of subjective, allegorical interpretation errors.

To the year and day, each of the fulfilled prophecies in the Old Testament about Jesus Christ came to pass as prophesied. According to God's appointed timeline, Jesus's birth, ministry, death, and resurrection literally occurred as the Old Testament predicted. There are no examples of non-literal fulfilments of any fulfilled prophecy given in the Bible. There is nothing subjective about prophecy. One can only assume that the prophecies we yet await for fulfilment will also come to pass literally.

The truth about the literal fulfilment of prophecy argues strongly for the literal method of interpretation. If a literal interpretation is not used in studying the scriptures, there is no objective standard to understand the Bible. Each person would be able to interpret the Bible as they saw fit. Biblical interpretation would devolve into "What the passage says to me." instead of "What the Bible intends to say." Sadly, this personal interpretive style is rampant with today's Bible study and teaching.

One of our goals, when studying the scriptures, should be to battle against our pride in our fallen state. Pride tempts us to think that our own views are always correct or that the beliefs of a particular teacher are flawless. No one has all the answers when it comes to interpreting the scriptures, even if they tell you they do. We must strive to be like the Bereans, who Luke commended for searching the scriptures daily to ensure that what Paul was teaching was accurate and true. We also need to apply this check and balance to our own perceived beliefs. *(Acts 17:11)*

Whenever we open the scriptures, we ought to seek guidance through prayer and the Holy Spirit for wisdom, discernment and guidance to lead us to accurate interpretation and understanding. The Bible does not require any mystical insight or extra logic to understand it; however, we are limited in our understanding. Only through study and prayer can we grow in the knowledge of the scriptures with God's blessing.

People often confuse the concept of interpretation with application of the scriptures. Although they are related, interpretation is different than application. When we interpret the Bible, we seek to understand what the text says and what the text means. Application follows interpretation. From understanding the text's literal meaning, we strive to apply what we learn to our lives.

One of the goals of studying the Bible is not to just fill our heads with knowledge but rather to apply the lessons to our daily living in obedience to God's directives for us as we strive to live Holy and blameless before him. Interpretation (meaning) is static, not allegorical. Application (applying the Word to our lives) is fluid and can convict each person according to their need.

(2 Corinthians 4:1-6)
"Therefore, having this ministry by the mercy of God, we do not lose heart. But we have renounced disgraceful, underhanded

One of the most significant errors when reading, teaching, or preaching the Bible is taking words, verses or paragraphs out of context. When we take a section of the text out of context, we can subvert, distort or completely change the author's meaning and intended learning for the reader. Taking verses out of context has the grave potential of creating a false Gospel, interpretive error, misunderstanding, misapplication, and distorted or heretical theology.

So what does it mean to read in context? There are seven principles of context to take into consideration when interpreting the text you are reading. Again, this might sound daunting, but it is not. You passively practice at least some of these principles every day when you read or study any material. Let's take a look at each principle and how you employ it when studying the Word.

Principle One: Literary Meaning. We will want to seek to understand what the author is saying and conveying to the reader in a literal sense. We have extensively covered literal, interpretive reading and understanding in the above paragraphs.

Principle Two: Cultural/Historical Setting. Who is the text addressing? How would it have been understood at the time of writing? Learning how cultures differ from the day of writing and today's modern culture helps us put the text into perspective. There are two main groups addressed in the New Testament scriptures. Jews and Gentiles. These two groups are further broken down into two categories: those that believe in Christ and those that do not. In the scriptures, you have believers and unbelievers in each group. It is essential to understand what group is being addressed and what their position in Christ is. One great example of this principle is (Revelation 7:4)

(Revelation 7:4)
"And I heard the number of those who were sealed. One hundred and forty-four thousand of all the tribes of the children of Israel were sealed:" (NKJV)

This verse goes on to say that the 144,000 are comprised of 12,000 from each of the 12 tribes of Isreal and names the tribes. It then tells us that God will seal and anoint this group of messianic believers to evangelize the nations in the tribulation. The verse is clear, precise and very specific. It has nothing to do with the gentiles and nothing to do with the church. There is no reason whatsoever not to read this in a literal sense. Unfortunately, most of today's teachers allegorize this verse to mean anything other than what it literally teaches and attempt to apply it to the church or spiritualize it.

One of many arguments they put forth is to allegorize the verse to represent something other than what it says because the twelve tribes are no longer intact, so it can't happen. Are you kidding me? You don't think our omnipotent, omnipresent, all-powerful God, the creator of the heavens and earth and everything in it, cannot pluck these folks out and mark them as His for His purpose? This is a perfect example of why literalism coupled with historical context and who is being addressed is essential for accurate interpretation.

Principle Three: The Type of Book. What type of book you are reading will determine how it is put into context. We have extensively covered the book types in chapter 3. You will handle a book of history differently than you will handle a book of prophecy or poetry and so on.

Principle Four: Grammer. Considering the tense, the word meaning, the plurality, and the sentence structure will help contextualize the verse correctly. Exegesis is the critical fundamental here, as we looked at earlier.

Principle Five: Micro Text. Looking at the micro text or the text immediately preceding and immediately following the verse will give you a clearer understanding of its context. Scripture is not a collection of sound bites to read independently of the entirety of the text.

Principle Six: Macro Text. Looking at the surrounding paragraphs and book theme will give you a clearer understanding of its context. Expanding this view through the entirety of the scriptures gives you an even clearer perspective and understanding. The Bible first, is the collective story of our creator addressing His creation and telling His story. The narrative transitions into the story of redemption, victory over sin, and ultimately to our redeemer and our salvation in Christ through Him. The scriptures glorify God from beginning to end. We always want to keep this in mind and at the forefront of our thoughts when studying the Word.

(1 Thessalonians 2:13)
"And we also thank God continually because, when you received the word of God, which you heard from us, you accepted it not as a human word, but as it actually is, the word of God, which is indeed at work in you who believe."

Considering the Bible in this macro context, we begin to mature in our faith and better understand the redemptive story and salvation as we study the Bible. We begin to understand our fallen state and see the sin in our lives better highlighted. Our hearts begin to ache for the lost, and we yearn to share Jesus with them. Jesus is woven throughout the Testaments, both Old and New. We begin to recognize God in the human experience as Father, Son and Holy Spirit and how each member of the Godhood interacts with both humanity and the Word.

Each of the Books in the Bible, woven into this cohesive story, takes us down the road to the beginning of wisdom and knowledge. It is a marvellous journey of discovery! Each word, verse, chapter, and book taken in its literary context, and the greater macro context, increase the Word's clarity and understanding. As we study, absorb, and mature in our faith, the Word becomes active and living within us, judging our attitude and heart.

(Hebrews 4:12)
"For the word of God is alive and active. Sharper than any double-edged sword, it penetrates even to dividing soul and spirit, joints and marrow; it judges the thoughts and attitudes of the heart."

As we looked at before, all scripture is God-breathed and is useful for teaching, rebuking, correcting, and training in righteousness to equip the believer. Not just our favourite verses.

(2 Timothy 3:16-17)
"All Scripture is God-breathed and is useful for teaching, rebuking, correcting and training in righteousness, so that the servant of God may be thoroughly equipped for every good work."

Principle Seven: Comparative Study. Bible interpretation often fails when we isolate a single concept without considering other verses of the same concept. Often, it is a collaboration of verses that gives us the clear teaching of the scriptures. Without taking the entirety of the teaching on a subject found throughout the Bible, we can develop a misunderstood, misleading and false understanding of what is taught. This failure leads to the claim that the scriptures are contradictory. They are not, never were and never will be.

Only when we read the scriptures literally, and in context, in their entirety, and understand who is being addressed do we have complete clarity. Was the text written to the Jews, the Jewish Nation, the Church, the Christians, the Gentiles, a conflagration of groups or an individual? Is the text discussing past, current or future events? Is the text informational, instructive, rebuking or corrective? These questions matter to contextualize and correctly interpret and apply the teaching.

It has been said (I am not sure who first said it.) That context is King. Follow this rule, and you will be well on your way to correctly handling the Word of Truth.

Chapter Six
FALSE PROPHETS/TEACHERS

You might ask, what does learning about false prophets, teachers, false preachers, and heretics have to do with learning how to study the Bible effectively? Once again, a lot. Your primary study should always be, first and foremost, the Bible. Your secondary or complementary study and learning will come from secondary sources. With these secondary sources, you need to exercise caution because they can lead you astray from the truth of the Word.

Your secondary sources of study can be any or all of the following—books, teachers, mentors, commentaries, dictionaries, lexicons, internet searches, videos, sermons, lectures, conferences, and so on. In both the Old and New Testaments, guarding against false prophets and teachers is common teaching. In fact, almost every New Testament book repeatedly warns against falling into the trap of being deluded and deceived by these sheep in wolves' clothing. If you happen to pick a source that teaches a false or misleading Gospel or distorts scriptural truth, you need to flee from this. As usual, our instruction will be taken directly from the scriptures.

(1 Timothy 6:3-5)

"If anyone teaches a different doctrine and does not agree with the sound words of our Lord Jesus Christ, and with the doctrine and teaching which is in agreement with godliness (personal integrity, upright behavior), he is conceited and woefully ignorant [understanding nothing]. He has a morbid interest in controversial questions and disputes about words, which produces envy, quarrels, verbal abuse, evil suspicions, and perpetual friction between men who are corrupted in mind and deprived of the truth, who think that godliness is a source of profit [a lucrative, money-making business—withdraw from them]." (AMP)

(Matthew 7:15-16)

"Beware of the false prophets, [teachers] who come to you dressed as sheep [appearing gentle and innocent], but inwardly are ravenous wolves. By their fruit you will recognize them [that is, by their contrived doctrine and self-focus]. Do people pick grapes from thorn bushes or figs from thistles?" (AMP)

Ok, great, we know we need to avoid being deceived by false teachers, but how do we accomplish this? It just so happens there are many scriptural tests to apply to teaching and teachers to sift the tares from the wheat, the good from the bad, the godly from the ungodly. However, the first requirement is to know the Word and be prepared to defend your faith in season and out of season. To have your feet fitted with the readiness that comes from the Gospel of peace. Our desire should be to know the Word and be a doer of the Word as we are admonished to do in the scriptures.

Although I could simply give you a list of false teachers and false books that pervert and twist the scriptures, I will not do that. There is a saying that goes, "Give a man a fish, and you will feed him for a day. Teach a man to fish, and he can feed himself for a lifetime." I am not sure who originally wrote that saying; several folks claim to be the originator, but it is full of wisdom and practicality. I am going to take the same approach with this chapter. There is not a lot of value in a list of folks to avoid because that list would only be a temporary band-aide.

Scriptures teach that there will be a great apostasy and a plethora of false teachers continually popping up to deceive you in these last days. If you simply receive a list today, it will be inadequate for tomorrow and beyond because these charlatans keep popping out of the woodwork and coming onto the scene daily and weekly. You will need a new list next week and then another new list the week after that. It is only going to get worse. Only when you have the skillset to

discern the Godly teachers from the un-Godly ones
on your own can you protect and guard yourself
against the apostasy and the falsehood these deceivers
spew.

(2 Peter 2:1-2)
*"But false prophets also arose among the people, just as there
will be false teachers among you, who will secretly bring in
destructive heresies, even denying the Master who bought them,
bringing upon themselves swift destruction. And many will
follow their sensuality, and because of them the way of truth will
be blasphemed."*

(1 Timothy 4:1-2)
*"The Spirit clearly says that in later times some will abandon
the faith and follow deceiving spirits and things taught by
demons. Such teachings come through hypocritical liars, whose
consciences have been seared as with a hot iron."*

The first warning sign of a false teacher, prophet,
preacher or heretic is evident by what they are
teaching. From this point forward, I will refer to this
group of four as just false teachers. If they teach a
different Gospel than what we find in the Bible, they
are false teachers. If their words contradict what is
taught by Jesus and the Bible authors, they are false
teachers. If they change, omit, add, or remove words,

verses, or passages to fit their theology, they are false teachers. If they teach that there are contradictions or errors in the Bible, they are false teachers. If they deny Christ's or the Holy Spirits Deity, they are false teachers. If they spiritualize or allegorize sections of the Bible that are clearly literal teachings, they are false teachers. They are false teachers if they ignore Bible truths to appease or condone a specific societal group engaged in sinful, immoral behaviours or actions contrary to Bible teaching.

For most of the issues in the above paragraph, a reference check against the scriptures is all that is required. It is easy to determine if words, verses, or paragraphs have had the original intent of the author conveying altered or removed. It is also easy to determine if a teacher contradicts or claims there are contradictory items in the Bible. They will come right out and tell you there are. It is also easy to spot false teachers who condone and even promote immorality and immoral lifestyles the Bible speaks out against. Here again, you simply test what they are teaching against the Word. If the Word says don't yet they say do, flee from this teacher. If the teaching is false and misguided, you will know it right away as you become more familiar with the Bible. Like I mentioned before. A Bible teacher does not get to change, alter or distort the Word of God because they do not like what it is saying, teaching, or speaking out against. Like the Bereans, search the scriptures daily to test what is being taught against the Word. *(Acts 17:11)*

(2 Timothy 4:3-4)
"For the time is coming when people will not endure sound teaching, but having itching ears they will accumulate for themselves teachers to suit their own passions, and will turn away from listening to the truth and wander off into myths."
(ESV)

Many cults and false teachers have one major item in common. They add their own concocted heresies to their teaching by claiming they have received some form of divine revelation, message or inspiration directly from God that are exclusive to them. These purported divine revelations can come in the form of objects, writings, dreams, visions and so on. Of course, these discoveries are usually purported to be too Holy for anyone to look upon them. Or for anyone to be a witness to the creation or receiving of these items or events. There is a surprise.

(1 John 4:1)
"Beloved, do not believe every spirit, but test the spirits to see whether they are from God, for many false prophets have gone out into the world." (ESV)

The founder of one popular group claims an angel directed him to an undisclosed location to receive a new revelation from God. A set of golden plates, or a golden-leafed book, that contains a new revelation. Of course, no one but the finder could look at this discovery on the penalty of death. It is interesting to know that this individual was also convicted several times of being a con-man and that he had been arrested upwards of 42 times. This group now uses this transcribed "New" book as a companion book equal to the authority of the Bible. The actual existence of this golden book has never been verified. (And never will be.) You would think this might raise more than an eyebrow or two. However, hundreds of thousands of people have been duped and deceived by this "New" discovery since 1830 and continue to be led astray from the one true Gospel today.

In the late 1800s, another false teacher decided he did not like or agree with the teachings of the Presbyterian church he was attending and set out to redefine accepted Bible interpretation. What resulted was mind baffling translations of basic Christian tenets and doctrines. This new teaching denies the Deity of Christ, claims only 144,000 people will be heavenly resurrected and that the balance of Christians await an earthly resurrection. The Holy Spirit is not a member of the Godhood. The Jews built the Egyptian pyramids under God's direction, the second coming has invisibly taken place, and Christ is now ruling the earth from his heavenly throne. I could go on and on, but I will not. Simply bizarre. There are millions and millions of pieces of literature printed by this group and consumed by unsuspecting people that are being led astray even today. The converts of this group go door to door, perpetuating the lies and deceit they offer. Once again, hundreds of thousands of people have been duped by this deceptive teaching and misapplication of the scriptures.

(2 Corinthians 11:13-15)
"For such men are false apostles, deceitful workmen, disguising themselves as apostles of Christ. And no wonder, for even Satan disguises himself as an angel of light. So it is no surprise if his servants, also, disguise themselves as servants of righteousness. Their end will correspond to their deeds." (ESV)

One famous modern-day preacher, a best-selling author, claims that an angel came to her and told her to write down a whole host of revelations he would dictate to her and get this new teaching out to the masses. "Ah, no, an angel did not, and you are a charlatan." Some claim to have made the trip to heaven to chat with God or Jesus and now have a new enlightened message for us. "Ah, no, you did not and do not. You are all charlatans." Some have claimed they have been given an exclusive insight into the day and hour of the Lord's return and then published this data. Of course, this day comes and goes, and they are still here. "Ah, no, you were not given any exclusive insight because you are a false teacher. No one knows the day or the hour except the Father, as scriptures teach." The list of fanciful claims coming out of these posers pretending to be servants of God is astounding. What is more astonishing is that people are falling for these deceptions and eating them up.

The bottom line on this one is to test all teaching against the Word. Guard yourself against falsehood. Flee from anyone that distorts, changes, misrepresents, adds to, or takes away from scripture. Look the other way when anyone is claiming personal revelation that has come only to them to share with the world. Scripture teaches the word of God is not of private interpretation. Only you can keep yourself from being deceived with false teaching and preaching.

(2 Peter 1:20-21)
"But understand this first of all, that no prophecy of Scripture is a matter of or comes from one's own [personal or special] interpretation, for no prophecy was ever made by an act of human will, but men moved by the Holy Spirit spoke from God." (AMP)

The scriptures would not have spent so much time addressing this issue of heresy and heretics if God did not want you to protect yourself against it. Doing a little research into a person or group goes a long way in determining both their validity and doctrine or lack thereof. Seeking the advice and opinion of Godly men and women that you trust in the Word can also help in this area. With prayer, meditation, beseeching the Holy Spirit, and study, know the Word. Walk in wisdom and understanding. Flee from heresy.

The next thing you will want to examine is the fruit of the teacher or ministry you are in or considering. As we see in the passage from Matthew 17:15-16 we looked at above, Scripture teaches us that we will know false teachers, preachers, and heretics by their fruit. Are they teaching a self-centred, self-focused Gospel or is their teaching Christ-centered and Christ-focused. Does their church or ministry feel more like an hour of entertainment than a time of worship and reverence for God? If you are more inclined to have a box of popcorn and soda pop in this environment than a Bible and a spirit of worship, run. We go to church to worship God and build each other up in our faith through fellowship, ministry, evangelism, and discipleship. The purpose of the Church is not to entertain you. It is not about you. It is about God and showing reverence to Him.

(James 3:1)
"Not many [of you] should become teachers [serving in an official teaching capacity], my brothers and sisters, for you know that we [who are teachers] will be judged by a higher standard [because we have assumed greater accountability and more condemnation if we teach incorrectly]." (AMP)

If the teacher or church leader is on stage slapping people around, pretending to heal them and putting on a good show, run. If they are stopping mid-sentence, cocking their ear to the heavens and start having a supposed two-way audible conversation with God, Run. If leaders are teaching people to flop around on the ground like beached whales gnashing their teeth, run. The only scriptural evidence I see of this is people filled with demons. This type of environment is more akin to a comedy show than a house of worship. When I witness this junk, I actually laugh out loud before I cry and pray for these lost souls leading people and themselves to their doom.

If there is strife and continuing scandal and division within the leadership, run. If the leadership is not above and beyond reproach, Run. If the leadership is not exhibiting Spirit-filled Christ-centred lives, Run. Those who lead the Church are called to a higher calling and are expected to be beyond reproach. You are being deceived. These leaders are not of God, and they seal their fate in apostasy. One day they will stand before God and give an accounting. It will not go well for them.

(1 Timothy 3:2)
"Therefore an overseer must be above reproach, the husband of one wife, sober-minded, self-controlled, respectable, hospitable, able to teach," (ESV)

(Romans 16:17)
"I appeal to you, brothers, to watch out for those who cause divisions and create obstacles contrary to the doctrine that you have been taught; avoid them." (ESV)

(Acts 20:28-30)

"Therefore take heed to yourselves and to all the flock, among which the Holy Spirit has made you overseers, to shepherd the church of God which He purchased with His own blood. For I know this, that after my departure savage wolves will come in among you, not sparing the flock. Also from among yourselves men will rise up, speaking perverse things, to draw away the disciples after themselves." (NKJV)

The next area to look at is an easy one. There is a multitude of charlatans out there posing as men of God that are singularly focused on lining their own pockets and enriching themselves at the expense of others with the Gospel. You cant even call these people Christian, for they are not, but they do a fantastic job of fleecing unsuspecting people out of their money for personal gain. I am always amazed at how gullible and susceptible people are to these deceivers and thieves. These criminals have no qualms in taking the last of the downtrodden, widows and poor folk's money. They actively seek to dupe these poor souls out of it.

Most of these charlatans will misinterpret and misrepresent the passage from either (Luke 21:1-4) or (Mark 12:41:44) to steal from the poor.

(Luke 21:1-4)

"As Jesus looked up, he saw the rich putting their gifts into the temple treasury. He also saw a poor widow put in two very small copper coins. "Truly I tell you," he said, "this poor widow has put in more than all the others. All these people gave their gifts out of their wealth; but she out of her poverty put in all she had to live on."

On the surface of this passage, you might assume Jesus is chastising the rich and commending the poor widow. This might very well be so, but it is not the teaching here. Only when you take the verse in context to include the pre-text and post-text surrounding these verses, do you get the complete and actual picture. In the verse before this passage, Jesus condemns the religious leaders for stealing from widows and the poor and for hypocrisy that would improvise. Before this, in chapter 7 of Mark, Jesus takes to task the religious leaders that would improvise others. The post-text describes this fleecing as vain because the temple will soon be brought down to rubble.

The sure tell sign of a charlatan and thief is to look at how they enrich themselves at your and the church's expense. Do they have three Mercedes and a

Bently outside their 10 million dollar mansion with three swimming pools and a tennis court? Do they own several private jets that whisk them to one of their many private vacation estates? Do they look like the Kardashians, all bobbled up with gold and diamonds and silk suits and dresses? If any of these things are evident, they are not men or women of God.

1 Timothy 6:5
"and perpetual friction between men who are corrupted in mind and deprived of the truth, who think that godliness is a source of profit [a lucrative, money-making business—withdraw from them]." (AMP)

2 Peter 2:3
"And in their greed they will exploit you with false arguments and twisted doctrine. Their sentence [of condemnation which God has decreed] from a time long ago is not idle [but is still in force], and their destruction and deepening misery is not asleep [but is on its way]. (AMP)"

(Titus 1:11)
"They must be silenced, because they are upsetting whole families by teaching things they should not teach for the purpose of dishonest financial gain." (AMP)

There is nothing wrong with wealth if you have not become beholden to money, and it has not become your God. There are many scriptural examples of Godly people whom God has blessed. The difference between Biblical blessing and self-enrichment is how you get the cash. The Biblical method is by blessing and provision from God. The charlatans' process is by dupping and deceiving people from their hard-earned money for personal gain under the guise of religion.

Today's charlatans engage in the same practice as those Jesus was chastising. They will suck anybody and everybody dry for their personal financial gain. If you see one of these folks trying to sell you a bag of Holy water for ten or so bucks, run. If you see them promising a financial blessing if you will donate so many dollars, run. If they spend more time begging and guilting you into donating than they do preaching, run. If they are offering membership into an exclusive club with a badge of honour of platinum, gold, silver or bronze level memberships that you display, run. If they call out and praise large donators, run. Our giving is to be in secret. Our left hand should not know what our right hand is doing. If we give publically, for public praise, our reward is from man's admiration rather than from God, and there is no Godly reward. Your giving should be in secret and not for all to see.

(Matthew 6:1-4)

"Be careful not to practice your righteousness in front of others to be seen by them. If you do, you will have no reward from your Father in heaven. "So when you give to the needy, do not announce it with trumpets, as the hypocrites do in the synagogues and on the streets, to be honored by others. Truly I tell you, they have received their reward in full. But when you give to the needy, do not let your left hand know what your right hand is doing, so that your giving may be in secret. Then your Father, who sees what is done in secret, will reward you."

All of this does not mean faithful men of God preaching and teaching the Word should not receive fair and reasonable compensation for their work. They should, as scripture teaches. There is a big difference between providing for the worker and the working enriching themselves beyond measure through deception, stealing from the poor with criminal motivation. Be a good steward of your money and try not to get duped by the charlatans. You will be better off supporting those in need directly. Avoid these folks as you mature and draw near to the Our Lord Jesus as they will lead you astray.

1 Timothy 5:18
"For the Scripture says, "You shall not muzzle the ox while it is treading out the grain [to keep it from eating]," and, "The

worker is worthy of his wages [he deserves fair compensation].”
(AMP)

In addition to the above, guard yourself against any group or movement that claims it is a "New" movement or a "New" revelation. As before, I am not going to call these groups out here as you must have the ability to recognize them. All of these "New" groups or teachings are always led by a false teacher. Now that you know how to pick these charlatans out of a crowd, it will be easy to recognize their heretical teachings and the groups or movements they have established. They are numerous.

These false groups or movements have one element in common. They all minimize the power and majesty of God. They put God In a box to be summoned at their will and their beck-and-call. Like a genie in a bottle, a little rub and out God will pop to grant all their wishes. Their teachings are heretical and have absolutely nothing to do with the scriptures. Their movements and teaching contradict what the Bible teaches. You can find many good books written by Godly authors that address the teaching of the heresies they espouse and put forward. Each one demands a complete book of their own to call them out.

If you hear any of the following terms, run:

Prosperity Gospel.
Name it and claim it.
Replacement theology.
New age spirituality.
Interfaith dialogue.
Word of Faith movement.
Progressive/Liberal Christianity.
Christian Science.
Positive confession movement.

To name just a couple of these heretical movements. Like false teachers, new ones pop up weekly. Only through a thorough knowledge of the scriptures and testing these heresies against what the Word of God teaches will you know to flee. They are wolves and deceivers inspired by Satan to strip you of the one true Gospel of Jesus Christ.

(2 Corinthians 11:12-15)
"But what I do, I will also continue to do, that I may cut off the opportunity from those who desire an opportunity to be regarded just as we are in the things of which they boast. For such are false apostles, deceitful workers, transforming themselves into apostles of Christ. And no wonder! For Satan himself transforms himself into an angel of light. Therefore it is no great

This chapter is a foundational teaching in recognizing false teachers and heretics for you to build on. It is not exhaustive but rather instructional. I encourage you to test all teaching against the words of Scripture and our Lord Jesus. To use the test of reasonableness and comparative study to sift falsehood from truth. Only you can guard yourself against these wolves we are told, are, and will, come amongst us, only getting worse as time marches on.

Chapter Seven
HOW TO MEMORIZE THE BIBLE

Memorizing scripture is one of the greatest privileges and goals the Christian can aspire to achieve. It is an integral part of the Christian life and, dare I say, a necessity to grow and mature in your faith, draw near to God, gain wisdom and understanding, train in righteousness, renew our minds, live in obedience to the Word, witness effectively to others, encourage believers, give a defence of your faith, keep us from sin and temptation, correction, combat the lies and attacks of that great deceiver Satan and his minions, guard ourselves against heresies and false teaching, and be blessed by God. Each of these reasons to memorize God's Word, along with many more, are found throughout the scriptures.

Oh, my goodness, that is a mouthful but only scratches the surface. Consider, if you will, the possibility that you decide to head into the mountains to do a little mining for gold. You get your sifting tray ready, prepare a snack and head out to your favourite little stream. Once there, you start to sift, and in your first tray, you pull out more gold than you have ever seen. Tray after tray, the gold just keeps coming. So much so, you are going to have a hard time packing it down the mountain. When you finally take a break and sit down for your snack, you notice a glint in the rock beside you. With a bit of inspection, you see that you are sitting in the middle of a diamond field. You forget your snack and gold and start cracking rocks, pulling out diamond after diamond. Due to your state of euphoria, you do not even notice the sun is setting as you continue to labour away. What is going through your mind during this adventure?

Some will be shouting at the top of their lungs with joy. Others might start planning how to spend this mountain of loot planning on a new house, a new car, a vacation property and more. Others will be making plans to solve all of their family and friends' financial woes. Still, others might wonder how this has been possible and why me. One thing all will have in common is the knowledge that they have come across the most incredible riches known to man, and it is in their hands and at their disposal. You will notice in this example that some are going to use this newfound wealth to enrich themselves and some to enrich others. The third person considers why they have been chosen for this financial blessing.

I have some good news and bad news. The bad news, if by chance, you were the one to come across this incredible wealth, it is temporal. You can not take it with you when you go, and it will most likely lead you down a path of temptation and sin, catching you up in the ways of this world. We are not to love the world or anything in the world, including riches. It does not say we can not achieve riches. It says not to love them. We are admonished in the scriptures to guard ourselves against the lust of the flesh, the lust of the eyes, and the pride of life. This find might not have been the blessing we supposed.

(1 John 2:15-17)
"Do not love the world or anything in the world. If anyone loves the world, love for the Father is not in them. For everything in the world—the lust of the flesh, the lust of the eyes, and the pride of life—comes not from the Father but from the world. The world and its desires pass away, but whoever does the will of God lives forever."

On the other hand, the good news is, these supposed riches are nothing compared to the riches available to you right now! The Bible declares that God's decrees (the Word of God) are more precious than pure gold and sweeter than the honey from the honeycomb and that His Word will endure forever.

(Psalm 19:9-10)
"The fear of the Lord is pure, enduring forever.
The decrees of the Lord are firm, and all of them are righteous.
They are more precious than gold, than much pure gold;
they are sweeter than honey, than honey from the honeycomb."

The Word of God is profitable for each one of its values listed in the first paragraph and many more. The everlasting truth of the Word provides all the riches you will ever need. It is the most spectacular thing that you will ever make as part of your life. We are admonished to write the Book (Memorize it) of the Law, God's Word, in our hearts and in our minds and meditate on it day and night. It is to dwell in us richly, teaching, admonishing, imparting wisdom, and spoken out loud with thankfulness in our hearts.

Joshua 1:8
"This Book of the Law shall not depart from your mouth, but you shall meditate on it day and night, so that you may be careful to do according to all that is written in it. For then you will make your way prosperous, and then you will have good success." (ESV)

Colossians 3:16
"Let the word of Christ dwell in you richly, teaching and admonishing one another in all wisdom, singing psalms and

hymns and spiritual songs, with thankfulness in your hearts to God." (ESV)

Not only do the scriptures repeatedly tell us in both Testaments to know the Word, Love the Word, and be doers of the Word, Jesus and the New Testament authors set the example of why we need to know and memorize God's Word. There are 283 direct quotes of the Old Testament by the authors of the New Testament and an additional 494 paraphrased or referred references. One of the more famous stories that use Old Testament quotes is recounted in Matthew 4:1-11 about Jesus being tempted by Satan. It is such a great story and shows how important it is to know and have God's Word memorized that I will quote all of it below before we take a closer look at it.

(Matthew 4:1-11)

"Then Jesus was led by the Spirit into the wilderness to be tempted by the devil. After fasting forty days and forty nights, he was hungry. The tempter came to him and said, "If you are the Son of God, tell these stones to become bread." Jesus answered, "It is written: 'Man shall not live on bread alone, but on every word that comes from the mouth of God.'" Then the devil took him to the holy city and had him stand on the highest point of the temple. "If you are the Son of God," he said, "throw yourself down. For it is written: "He will command his angels

concerning you, and they will lift you up in their hands, so that you will not strike your foot against a stone.'" Jesus answered him, "It is also written: 'Do not put the Lord your God to the test.'" Again, the devil took him to a very high mountain and showed him all the kingdoms of the world and their splendor. "All this I will give you," he said, "if you will bow down and worship me." Jesus said to him, "Away from me, Satan! For it is written: 'Worship the Lord your God, and serve him only.'" Then the devil left him, and angels came and attended him."

I am confident that Jesus was not packing a complete set of Old Testament scrolls with him when he was led into the wilderness to be tempted by Satan with his scripture twisting offers. Can you imagine Satan making one of his offers and then Jesus saying, "Hold that thought, Satan, let me see if I can look up a verse somewhere in these scrolls here to find a good answer." No, Jesus combatted Satan with the Word of God by knowing the Word of God and having it written in his heart and mind. The significant number of New Testament examples quoting the Old Testament follows this same thought of the verses being known (Memorized), not looked up. We are to strive to be Christ-like and to learn and follow from his words and example. Memorizing God's Word is one of these areas to be like our Lord.

Not only did Jesus and the Testament writers know the scriptures, Jesus rebuked the Sadducees in Matthew 22 for not knowing the scriptures. The Sadducees come to Jesus questioning him about a woman who has become a widow seven times and whose wife she will be in the resurrection. The Sadducees did not believe in the resurrection. Rather than first answering the question, Jesus takes them to task for not knowing the scriptures or the power of God. He deals with their misinterpretation and incorrectly handling the word of truth because they did not know and accept the Word from the Old Testament scrolls they purported were the teachers and keepers of. Once he rebukes them for not accepting the resurrection or, as He put it, "The power of God," he then goes on to answer their question.

We know the scriptures by writing them within us (Memorizing them), accepting them as written (Not allegorizing), and then wielding them daily (Recalling, reciting and applying them), for all of the reasons given in the first paragraph of this chapter. I am not talking about simple head knowledge but writing them deep within your being to apply with faith to the daily circumstances you find yourself in—have a deep, life-altering love for the Word of God. I could fill this whole chapter with verses on memorizing and the importance of memorizing the scriptures; however, I will just quote a couple.

(Deuteronomy 11:18)
"You shall therefore lay up these words of mine in your heart and in your soul, and you shall bind them as a sign on your hand, and they shall be as frontlets between your eyes." (ESV)

(Psalm 119:11)
"I have stored up your word in my heart, that I might not sin against you." (ESV)

(Proverbs 6:21-22)
"Bind them on your heart always; tie them around your neck. When you walk, they will lead you; when you lie down, they will watch over you; and when you awake, they will talk with you." (ESV)

(Ephesians 6:15)
"and with your feet fitted with the readiness that comes from the gospel of peace."

(1 Peter 3:15)
"But in your hearts honor Christ the Lord as holy, always being prepared to make a defense to anyone who asks you for a

The scriptures are clear, and there is no grey area or misunderstanding of God's expectation of us when it comes to memorizing His Word. We are to write God's word within our hearts and minds. We are commanded to memorize it and be prepared to give a defence of our faith, evangelize others, meditate on it and achieve and execute all of those items and more, as listed in the first paragraph of this chapter. Ok, great, now that we are aware of the expectation, where do we go from here? How am I ever going to achieve this?

Most people, I am not sure of the percentage, but I am sure it is in the '90s, tell me they are awful at memorizing. They find it to be an impossible task. My answer back to them is it is all a matter of importance, perspective, expectation and effort. Memorization takes work and dedication to achieve, but the result is obedience to God's instructions and blessings beyond measure. It is more than worth the effort. You will not read a passage or verse through once or even five times and then have that verse committed to memory for life. Like any skill you learn in life, memorization takes training, practice, time, and dedication to achieve.

When something is important to you, I am absolutely sure you make it happen. Whatever that critical something is, the greater the level of importance it is to you, the higher you place it on your list of things to get done. The items of the most significant importance are placed at the top of your task list. These items get completed. Those items with less importance get pushed down to the bottom. Some lower-priority items never make it back up again. Only when you place the memorization of the scriptures at or near the top of your list will you make progress. Memorization is a daily, lifelong pursuit.

When you perceive you are unable to do something, you will probably never be able to achieve that something. What prevents most people from learning a new skill or being successful with an unfamiliar task is the fear of failure. They have convinced themselves it is an impossible task. With the proper training and support, you can accomplish anything, including memorizing the scriptures. When you change your perception of a task from impossible to probable, you can and will be successful. It starts with believing you can rather than you perceiving you cant. Change your perspective from one of failure to success. Only then will you have the mindset to be successful with the great pleasure of memorizing the scriptures.

Setting a reasonable expectation of yourself is also paramount for success in anything you do, including learning and memorizing God's word. If you commit to learning the entirety of the psalms in a week, well, that is ridiculous, and you will never achieve this goal unless you have a photographic memory. Most of us do not. Knowing the scriptures is like having a great meal—one bite at a time. You would never lift a full plate of food to your lips and try to inhale the whole thing in one gulp. You would choke, spill it all over yourself and not enjoy the experience. You eat your meal one enjoyable bite at a time, savouring each mouthful before taking the next. When it is complete, if you are like me, you will take a big sigh of contentment and have a smile on your face. Memorizing the scriptures in this same way is paramount to success. Methodically, one piece at a time, savouring and absorbing each word and phrase as you write the Word within your mind and place it in your heart.

Learning and memorizing the scriptures takes time and effort. You will only get out what you put into it. No one masters a musical instrument, a profession or a sport without putting in the time and effort required. Those who become professionals and the best at what they do follow a controlled study, training, and repetitive process guided by a mentor or a coach to achieve success. They follow a dedicated program with detailed steps designed to improve their performance through to perfection progressively. You learn and memorize the scriptures in the same way. If you take a willy-nilly approach to achieve your goal with no planned program, plan, or performance measurement, you will not make significant progress.

Through this book, we have been looking at how not to do things as well as how to do them. One thing you want to avoid when working on your memorization program is comparing yourself to others. Doing this will only deflate you. We all learn and progress at a different pace. I am sure you know someone who rhymes off scripture left and right and appears to know more than they should. Look at these people as inspirations rather than stumbling blocks. They have probably been working on their memorization most of their lives, or at least a good portion of them. Memorizing the scriptures is not a race. If you can remember one verse a week, great. If you can memorize one passage a week, great. If you can memorize a chapter in a week, great. Next week, the only important thing is that you have more of God's Word written in your mind and on your heart than last week.

So how do we memorize the Word effectively? Some will teach many fancy terms and throw around a bunch of technical-sounding jargon, but let's keep it simple. Each of us has very different personalities and learning styles. Some learn visually, others learn audibly, seeing or listening or a combination of both. All memorization is accomplished by one form or the other. However, there are two advantages we all have for the very first critical steps down your journey to knowing the Word.

Step one – The Holy Spirit
(John 14:26)
"But the Helper (Comforter, Advocate, Intercessor— Counselor, Strengthener, Standby), the Holy Spirit, whom the Father will send in My name [in My place, to represent Me and act on My behalf], He will teach you all things. And He will help you remember everything that I have told you."
(AMP)

Step 2 - Prayer

(James 1:5-6)

"If any of you lacks wisdom [to guide him through a decision or circumstance], he is to ask of [our benevolent] God, who gives to everyone generously and without rebuke or blame, and it will be given to him. But he must ask [for wisdom] in faith, without doubting [God's willingness to help], for the one who doubts is like a billowing surge of the sea that is blown about and tossed by the wind." (AMP)

Well, there you go, you are halfway there! How easy was that? Ask the Holy Spirit for guidance, and he will help you remember everything that we have been told, the Word of God. Ask God in prayer in faith for wisdom, and He will generously give it to you without rebuke or blame, but you have to ask. These are two of the essential steps in our Christian life in all areas. Beseeching the Holy Spirit and prayer. And when we sit down to study, understand and memorize the Word, we need to take these two steps before God for his blessing and help with our endeavour.

Ok, now that you are halfway there, the rest is easy. Step three is to make a Study and memorization plan. I cannot make that plan for you because I don't know where you are in your Christian walk or if you have even started. The first verse every Christian usually learns is John (3:16)

(John 3:16)
"For God so loved the world that he gave his one and only Son, that whoever believes in him shall not perish but have eternal life."

Ok, great again, but where do we go from here? I keep referring to the opening paragraph of this chapter rather than repeating it in the body of the chapter but will need to refer you to it again. The items listed in the opening, like giving a defence of your faith, evangelizing, defeating the attacks of Satan and his minions in your life, in addition to all the others and more, are dealt with through the knowledge and recall of the scriptures.

To make a plan, determine what area in your life you want to first tackle with scripture memorization and then select appropriate scriptures to memorize. Do you want to begin with evangelism, spiritual warfare, in times of trouble and testing, the list goes on. You can use your favourite internet search engine or pick up a good memorization plan or program to select the verses. Once you have chosen some verses to memorize, get right down to the task. There is a multitude of methods you can employ. Here are some to consider that work well for me.

First, take it word by word. One of the very first groups of passages I memorized was the 6th chapter of Ephesians. This chapter gives instructions to children, parents, slaves (employees) and masters (Bosses). It then goes on from verses 10 to 20 to provide instruction on where our struggles come from and how to overcome them. Paul, the author of Ephesians, then finishes the chapter with an admonition to pray for both him and the saints. The section on spiritual warfare begins in verse 10. "Finally, be strong in the Lord and in His mighty power. Full stop. Here is the starting point. This is verses 10 of Ephesians 6. Now how to memorize it.

Understanding how the chapter is broken down, as I summarized above, is step one. Knowing the full context and meaning of the verses is the key to memorization. These are not just empty words you are trying to remember. Don't forget, the goal of memorizing the Word is so you can apply it and its use to your daily living. So the first thing you will want to do is study the text for its meaning and application before you even consider memorizing it. Once you have a feel for the context of the book, chapter, and paragraph your text is in, begin.

Looking at verse 10 teaches us to be strong in the Lord and rely on his strength, not our own. We are weak and feeble. God is almighty and powerful. Only through depending on Him and His power can we have victory, not of ourselves. Now, whenever we think and meditate on Ephesians 6:10, we can bring to mind victory through God and relying on His strength rather than our own. (Ephesians 6:10), "Finally, be strong in the Lord and in His mighty power." Once we understand the meaning in context and the takeaway from the verse, we get down to memorizing it. There is a multitude of methods you can use for memorization. Here is a couple of them.

The first thing I do is type the verse out multiple times in Word and then print it. I then cut out the verses and place them everywhere I usually travel around in a day. I put one in my pocket, one by my bed, one on the fridge, one in my office, one in my car and so on. I will frequently take the verse out of my pocket or glance at it when passing by a location and recite it, thinking about its meaning. Now, I will say, I now work on entire passages simultaneously, but you have to start somewhere. This is an excellent method and takes little time and effort. Before long, the verse will be instilled within your mind and in your heart forever.

Another method I use is to record the verse or passage in an audio file and put that audio file on my phone. Whenever I am completing a mundane task that does not take any concentration, I will play the verse or passage on repeat over and over, reciting it out loud and meditating on it as it plays. I will also use this method to lull me off to sleep when having a snooze. When using any of these methods, I always include the book, chapter, and verse in the recall. Ex: (Ephesians 6:10) By learning the Book and chapter along with the verse, it helps you recall it once you know multiple scriptures.

Another method of memorizing scripture is to place yourself in the inverse of the text, formulating a question where the scripture verse is the answer. This helps your brain puzzle through the challenge of reorienting the verse. For example, Ephesians 6:10, I am weak and have no power. God is mighty and has all the power. What should I do? Now scripturalize the thought with the verse as the answer. I should (Ephesians 6:10) "Finally, be strong in the Lord and in His mighty power."

It is a good idea also to be frequently looking at the verse in your Bible. Not your phone, but your Bible. This helps you to have a visual representation of what it looks like and where it is in the text. Then, when you think about where to find the verse on being strong in the Lord, your brain will provide you with the visual picture. Oh ya, Ephesians 6:10, right-hand page upper middle. (In my Bible anyway). You can't get this same picture from your phone or tablet as the text is reflowable, meaning it changes size and position as you change fonts and font sizes or the device. Not to say you should not read your Bible on your phone or tablet. You should if you have these devices.

The last action I will take is to recite this verse as many times in a day as I can quietly to myself out loud once I know it. It will be my last thought before going to sleep and my first thought in the morning. Following these simple steps, there is no reason you cannot memorize at least one verse a day. Soon, with practice, prayer and the leading of the Spirit, you will be accomplishing whole passages in a day. Once I am confident I have seared the verse into my conscience, I will move on to the next verse. (Ephesians 6:11) "Put on the full armor of God, so that you can take your stand against the devil's schemes." Now I will follow the exact same process for this verse. Once complete, I will combine the two verses in my daily recall.

It makes no difference if it takes you a day or a week to memorize a verse. It is not a race. Be persistent until you have it. There is no need to rush. What you will find, as you spend more time doing it, you will quickly get better at it. Eventually, you will then move on to complete chapters and books. Although, when starting to memorize full Books of the Bible, I would recommend starting with a smaller book like Jude and then working up to the longer books. I am currently working on revelation and having a blast!

There are many tools you can use to help you read and memorize the Bible. Today you can purchase or get free electronic applications for your computer, smartphone or tablet. These apps can be complete Bible programs that you can read or listen to. They come in both plain and dramatized versions. They are an absolutely fantastic addition to any serious Bible student. The dramatized versions are enjoyable. You can also get lexicons, dictionaries, commentaries, study Bibles, and a whole host of secondary aids in electronic format. There are also many good Bible memory verse programs available both in print and electronically.

I would be remiss if I did not address the different Bible translations and which one you should read and memorize. This topic has always been a hot topic within the Christian denominations, and I am sure it will be until the Lord's return. Some claim only the Authorized King James Bible is the only accurate Bible and the only one you should read. On the other far end of the spectrum, others will claim the newer paraphrased editions are adequate because God is the one who ultimately reveals his word to you, and He can do so through these translations. This is now a personal opinion and not a direction so take from it what you will. I think both camps are off-base, and here is why.

Ultimately every translation from the King James to the living Bible is just that, a translation of the original. If you want to claim to be a purist, the only way to do that is to read the original scrolls in their original languages of Hebrew, Greek, and Aramaic. Period. This is beyond most of us. The King James proponents claim that it is the original English translation and the closest translation to the original scrolls. This is a misnomer. Although the King James is a great Bible, it is not the closest word-for-word translation to the original works or the first English-translated Bible.

The Tyndale Bible was the first English transcription from the original languages of the manuscripts and was completed in 1535. Although not considered as scripturally sound as the King James Bible initially transcribed in 1611, it was the first. The closest word-for-word translated Bible is the Interlinear Bible. This word interlinear means "a direct translation." So if you want to be the closest to an actual purist without using the originals, that would be it. Good luck using this one because Hebrew and Aramaic have nowhere near the grammatical structure English has, and it is almost impossible to decipher.

It is recognized that the New American Standard Bible (NASB) is the closest translation to the original languages that is somewhat legible in modern English, followed by the English Standard Version (ESV) and then bringing up third place the King James Version (KJV). The NIV is considered the closest accurate translation to our modern-day English and has taken into consideration the dead sea scroll discoveries. Each of these translations has strengths and weaknesses when compared to the original manuscripts, including the KJV. Sorry King James folks, no offence intended. I feel it is more dogma and tradition that keeps folks clinging to their chosen translation; however, there is nothing wrong with that. Each of these translations is absolutely fine as translations go.

On the other hand, there are a whole host of heretical works out there to avoid. If a translation does not include the entirety of the 66 Books, throw it out. For example, the Readers Digest Bible leaves out about 55% of the Old Testament and about 25% of the New Testament. I would also avoid Bible translations commissioned by the cults like the New World Translation (NWT) and others. Also, avoid any translations that add to, or take away from, the scriptures. As a general rule, the more current a translation, the more liberties they take and the more liberal they become. In some circumstances, they change the text's original genders, plurality, meaning, and intent. I would personally avoid any new translation or paraphrased translation of the Bible. I would also avoid any Bible transcribed by one person as this model has no accountability or checks and balances.

I personally believe it is best to choose a good, accepted as close to the original, accurate Bible translations like the KJV, ESV, NASB, NIV, or others for your daily reading and memorization. The differences in core meaning are minimal and are Doctrinally essentially identical. Pick one and stick with it. For in-depth Bible studies, I would read a combination of the Bibles paired with an Interlinear Bible, a good commentary, and an original languages lexicon. Now you are in the meat of the Word.

I could have spent the entirety of this book talking about the importance of memorizing the Bible. I have only scratched the surface on tips and tricks on how to learn the scriptures. Many people have developed many different methods. I like to keep things simple because that works for me. I have never been unable to successfully memorize a passage or Book with the techniques I have talked about above. If they do not work for you, develop your own or search out others. There are no rules. Just remember prayer and the leading of the Holy spirit are number one. Without the guidance of the Holy Spirit and prayer, you will miss out on the promises of help.

Love the Word! Know the Word! Be Thankful for the Word! Let the Word Dwell in you Richly! Be a Doer of the Word! And you will receive every good blessing in Christ!

(Colossians 3:16)
"Let the word of Christ dwell in you richly, teaching and admonishing one another in all wisdom, singing psalms and hymns and spiritual songs, with thankfulness in your hearts to God."

Chapter Eight
PUTTING IT ALL TOGETHER

To The Unsaved,

As you travel through this journey we call life; God sends many opportunities your way to come to know Him. Maybe it is people he sends across your path, a radio broadcast you "mistakenly" turned to, an internet website you "happened" upon, circumstances He brings or allows into your life, a book or a tract of some form and so on. God desires that all come to repentance and know Him and the saving grace of our Lord Jesus Christ.

(2 Peter 3:9)
"The Lord is not slow in keeping his promise, as some understand slowness. Instead he is patient with you, not wanting anyone to perish, but everyone to come to repentance."

If you have not accepted Jesus as your saviour, and are not yet a Christian, but have come across this book and are still here, just maybe this is one of the opportunities God is sending your way. I believe that ending up here was by design, and you are currently searching for truth and are being called by God. I can promise you with all my heart you have found the truth you are searching for. However, simply finding it is not enough; you have to do something with it.

Today, we have a systemic problem: many will reject God and salvation, citing the hypocrisy in those claiming Christ and the church. I completely understand this. Unfortunately, some within the church are posers, fakers, and imitation Christians who are not saved. This is no surprise, as God tells us this will be the case. There are also many heretics and false teachers spewing a false gospel, as we have already covered.

Matthew 13:30
"Let both grow together until the harvest. At that time I will tell the harvesters: First collect the weeds and tie them in bundles to be burned; then gather the wheat and bring it into my barn."

All of mankind, including you and me, are wretched sinners. Even our good works are but as filthy rags before God. This is why we need a Saviour and forgiveness. God tells us that breaking even the lest of his laws is punishable by death. In the style of Ray Comfort: Have you ever stolen anything, even a pencil? Have you ever taken the Lord's name in vain? Have you ever lusted after another person, even in your mind? Have you ever harboured hate for another person, even just a little? If you answered yes to these, an answer of no would be lying; you are a thieving, blaspheming, adulterous hateful person. Yup, I am guessing you are not as righteous as you thought. This is why we all need a saviour.

(Romans 3:23)
"for all have sinned and fall short of the glory of God,"

(Isaiah 64:6)
"But we are all like an unclean thing, And all our righteousnesses are like filthy rags; We all fade as a leaf, And our iniquities, like the wind, Have taken us away."

Don't let the failings of man and his institutions keep you from knowing the one true God and his Son Jesus Christ. Humankind will continually let you down until the return of the Lord and the abolishment of sin. My failings and the church's failings in no way nullify the existence, power and majesty of God our Creator, the Creator of the heavens and earth and all things in them.

For those that do not know Christ, the Bible and the message of the cross are foolishness. They are nothing but folly to be mocked and scoffed at. The scriptures tell us this. The Bible makes no sense and means nothing to the unsaved. Only through the Holy Spirit do we receive the gift of understanding and the gift of interpreting the Word of God correctly. Only through the acceptance of Jesus Christ as our saviour do we receive the ministry of the Holy Spirit to unravel the truth of God's Word. It is by God's grace alone that we become saved and not by works lest any man boast.

(1 Corinthians 1:18)
"For the message of the cross is foolishness to those who are perishing, but to us who are being saved it is the power of God."

(1 Corinthians 2:14)
"The person without the Spirit does not accept the things that come from the Spirit of God but considers them foolishness, and cannot understand them because they are discerned only through the Spirit."

So if you are on the fence, it is time to hop down and join the family of God. Only you can make this decision in your heart. No one can force or cajole you into it. The steps are easy. Confess before God that you are a sinner and that Jesus Christ paid the penalty for your sin by his death on the cross. Accept him as your Lord and Savior. Publically confess your faith in him and have true belief in your heart. If you have made a true confession, you will desire to share Christ with others, know his Word, and defeat sin in your life.

(Romans 10:8-9)
"But what does it say? "The word is near you; it is in your mouth and in your heart," that is, the message concerning faith that we proclaim: If you declare with your mouth, "Jesus is Lord," and believe in your heart that God raised him from the dead, you will be saved."

(Ephesians 2:8-9)
For it is by grace you have been saved, through faith—and this is not from yourselves, it is the gift of God— not by works, so that no one can boast.

(Acts 4:11-12)
"Jesus is the stone you builders rejected, which has become the cornerstone. Salvation is found in no one else, for there is no other name under heaven given to mankind by which we must be saved."

(John 14:6)
Jesus answered, "I am the way and the truth and the life. No one comes to the Father except through me."

Once you have taken these steps, get yourself a good Bible and start reading and memorizing it. Your life will begin to produce good fruit and works under God. The scriptures will come to life, and God will show you daily the wonders of his grace and power. From here, find a good Bible teaching believing church filled with the Spirit. Join in worship, and fellowship with believers of like mind and find a Godly mentor to help you on your journey.

If you are not ready to make a confession for Christ today, seek out people and resources who can answer your questions and help you along in your journey. But don't wait too long! The Lord will be returning for his Church very soon, maybe even today or tomorrow, and you do not want to miss the trip to heaven. Missing the trip means eternal separation from God in Hell, where there will be an eternity of weeping and gnashing of teeth. I would also be happy to answer any questions you have. You can reach out to me from the link to my website at the end of this chapter. May God grant you the wisdom to see and the desire within your heart to act on his calling.

To The Deceived,

If you are running around naming and claiming it, seeking riches with both feet in the world following the false teaching of the prosperity gospel, you are heading to an eternity of separation from God. If you are caught up in the New Age movements or Word of faith movements, or any of the other crazy trends out there, you are heading to an eternity of separation from God. Do you embrace the ecumenical movement that teaches all roads lead to God? If so, you are heading to an eternity of separation from God. Like any good stepped program, the first step is to understand and accept that you have been deceived. To realize that you are following a perverted and twisted gospel that has nothing to do with the actual scriptures.

We have extensively covered these false teachers and movements in the chapter on false prophets and teachers but as a reminder. If your movement puts God in a box for you to command at will, you are being deceived. If your movement promises all of the things the scriptures speak out against, you are being deceived. If your movement accepts and embraces sin, sinful or immoral lifestyles as defined in the scriptures, or condones any actions the Bible speaks out against, you are being deceived. The churches and heretical movements are full of deluded people who surround themselves with teachers willing to tell them whatever their itching ears want to hear to condone their immorality and sinful lifestyles.

(2 Timothy 4:3)
"For the time will come when people will not put up with sound doctrine. Instead, to suit their own desires, they will gather around them a great number of teachers to say what their itching ears want to hear."

Some will say that when you confess Jesus with your mouth, you are saved. Sorry, when you take all the scriptures together in context, that is not what the Bible teaches but only an incomplete piece of the steps to salvation. You need to confess with your mouth, believe in your heart, and accept that you are a wretched sinner and the price Christ paid for your sins with his death on the cross. This is the narrow road to salvation.

Many false confessions happen every day—mere lip service and not a true heartfelt belief. Many false Christs and false prophets will arise in these last days deceiving even the elect if that were possible, leading many astray producing false Christians. Many will claim Christ in Word only, but He does not know them as He himself says pretty harshly. Are you one of these posers? Are you on the broad road of destruction that most are heading down?

(Matthew 24:24)
"For false messiahs and false prophets will appear and perform great signs and wonders to deceive, if possible, even the elect."

(Matthew 7:13)
"Enter through the narrow gate. For wide is the gate and broad is the road that leads to destruction, and many enter through it."

(Matthew 7:22-24)
"Many will say to me on that day, 'Lord, Lord, did we not prophesy in your name and in your name drive out demons and in your name perform many miracles?' Then I will tell them plainly, 'I never knew you. Away from me, you evildoers!'

When you stand before the Lord on the day of judgement, will you hear, "I never knew you. Away from me, you evildoer!" or will you hear, "Well done, good and faithful servant."

The choice is yours. If you have recognized you are being deceived and are following a false movement, Christ, prophet, or teacher. Run. Like Lot and his family did, flee, and don't make the mistake of looking back. Find a Christ-centered, Spirit-filled, Bible-believing Church teaching the Word of God as it was written and intended to be taught. Find Christ in your heart and set your path straight. Then go forth correctly handling the Word of Truth. My prayers are with and for you!

To the Saved,

Great to have you in the family! See you at the Marriage Supper! If you feel this book might have any value for others, please consider directing them to it.

Thank you to all for spending this time with me. May this work be a blessing and a source of strength to you.
May God richly bless and keep you.
Grace and peace to you from Him who is, and who was, and who is to come.

Your humble servant in Christ,
Brian Cockell
I can be reached at <u>www.thenarrowway.ca</u>

Please feel free to reach out or stop in to say hi.

You will find my YouTube ministry videos on the site and my ministry blog, along with various items of

interest. If you join the site, you will be notified of my
subsequent two book releases when they become
available, as seen below.

COMING SOON

SO SORRY!
But you're not going to save it!

My new book, detailing, from a Biblical perspective, how this earth is on a collision course to disaster and the end of its existence.

The expected release date is Dec 2021.

&

TRIBULATION TRAINING!
Preparing for the end of days.
Goats to the left, sheep to the right please.

The end is nigh, and the Lord's return is imminent. Are you ready? A detailed scriptural walkthrough of how this world is marching towards the tribulation and what that means detailing the roles government, believers, unbelievers, and everyone in-between will play.

The expected release date is Jan 2022.